Tough at the Bottom

Mick O'Farrell

To the Soldier
from the Sailor.

Happy Christmas.
Martin
12/03.

Arriba Publications
Dublin 1999

Published in 1999 by

ARRIBA PUBLICATIONS,
7 Cowper Road, Rathmines,
Dublin 6.

© Arriba Publications
Cover by Sean De Paor
Cover Layout by Artwerk, Dublin.

Printed by ColourBooks

One
Cadet School

"Do you know what you remind me of?" the little corporal bellowed, his small wiry frame quivering with barely-suppressed fury, tiny droplets of spittle hanging in the crisp air as he warmed to his task.

Standing there rigidly in the snow, he surveyed the ten half-frozen members of No 5 Section with ill-concealed contempt, his words echoing hollowly back from the cluster of red-brick buildings surrounding the barracks square.

"I'll tell you what yez remind me of. Youse remind me of a seagull ... a great big fucking seagull, perched on the rim of a swill-barrel, looking down at the goodies below. Now he'd like to go down and get some, but he's afraid of being trapped. And so he keeps on teetering ... teetering" - he swayed backwards and forwards on his heels for effect - "teetering to and fro, his mind a complete ... fucking ... blank ..."

Just like yours, Cadet Smith!"

At that, Smithy woke up with a start. Smithy was one of those high IQ people who seem to exist in a world all of their own, but he also suffered from an unfortunate inability to keep in step when marching - when everybody else was up, he'd be down, leading one exasperated instructor to compare him to 'a worm in agony'.

It wasn't that Corporal Bagge was a wrong one - far from it. Like most of the Cadet School instructors, Billy was quite a decent fellow and we all parted on good terms later on, but after only a wet week in the army, how were we to know he was on probation as well and desperately keen to prove himself?

1

During a lull, we could hear the other four cadet sections being harangued in equally-colourful language by their own instructors, which provided a measure of perverse compensation - at least we knew everyone else was getting an equal bollocking. In the distance, Sgt. Jake Kelly's war-weary tones echoed back from the surrounding redbrick buildings.

"By the Lord Jaysus!" the pint-sized Jake intoned, shaking his head sadly. "I've met some duds in my time in the army, but youse lot take the fucking biscuit. But I'll make soldiers out of you yet even if it fucking-well kills me, which it probably fucking-well will!"

An NCO (non-commissioned officer) instructor in the Military College was a much-prized appointment demanding very high standards, and none of them, aside from a natural desire to see their own cadets do well, had any intention of going down the tubes because of our incompetence or stupidity. Regulations forbade the use of obscene language and were generally adhered to, but every now and again an instructor, under the most severe provocation, would lose the head completely and launch into some very choice language indeed, which could even be quite poetic at times.

Their use of the f-word was almost a work of art. They stuck it in the most unlikely places, in the middle of words, sentences, phrases, to lend flavour, emphasis. To army people, using it was like second nature and they never even seemed to notice. The head chaplain railed against it regularly from his pulpit on Sundays, horrified at the poor image it gave the army.

"My good man," he intoned piously to a blasphemous soldier one day. "If the f-word was banned, you'd be speechless." But all his efforts came to nought and not long afterwards he applied for a transfer to a more normal parish where such vulgarities were less commonplace.

A good deal of competition existed among the instructors, with each of them keen to see his own section become the best in the class, since any criticism of a cadet reflected badly on him. If the Commanding Officer, or CO for short, found a fault, he'd tick off the class officer, who'd then tick off the company sergeant, who in turn paraded the sergeants, who then abused the corporals, with everybody ending up giving the misfortunate cadets an unmerciful bollocking.

Over all loomed the menacing shadow of the sergeant major, known as the "Liver" Dunne because of his perpetual scowl and vile temper, who gloried in his reputation as 'the only NCO in the army with no friend but his mother'. As sergeant major, he was the main link between the commissioned and non-commissioned ranks and generally kept the whole show on the road. Glancing out the mess window one evening after duty hours, who should he spot but a newly-arrived red-arse cadet taking a short-cut straight across the barrack square, an unheard-of crime in those days. Lifting up the window with a crash, the Liver soon let him have a blast of his bile.

"Get off that fucking square, cadet," he roared. "Nobody crosses that square but dogs and officers."

The Liver was in total contrast to the company sergeant, Peter O'Connor, a burly tank of a Bargyman from New Ross in Wexford, possessed of all the good humour and manly honesty which marks that county's menfolk. Peter was the best rifle marksman in the entire army who could invariably put every one of his shots into a 4-inch square at 100 yards, and there was always a rush among the cadets to mark up his target on the shooting range in an effort to share in the reflected glory.

Originally a huge sprawl of wooden huts built by the British in the middle of the last century, the Curragh camp lies in the middle of a wide open plain dotted here and there with clumps of furze bushes, as flat and bare as the arctic tundra and damn near as cold in winter. Even in summer, the wind can whistle across the flat terrain in a manner that would skin a brass monkey and make even the hundreds of woolly sheep grazing there take shelter.

The present handsome red-brick buildings were completed around 1922, with the high water-tower, flying the national flag, dominating the surrounding flat plains. Three long parallel straight roads dissect the camp, running from east to west. Along the top road lie the officers messes, all seven of them, with the NCOs messes occupying the centre one, while the bottom road encompasses the married quarters, some shops, and the enlisted men's billets and canteens.

The Curragh itself is quite a famous place, celebrated in song and legend by both singer Christy Moore and the tale of the King of Leinster and St. Brigid, who wished to establish a religious order in Kildare in the 5th century. As a reward for banishing his ass's ears, Brigid was offered any wish she desired by the king and chose as much ground for her cell as she could get, so she threw her cloak out and it spread and spread till it covered the entire Curragh plain, a pretty vast expanse by any standards. The king's reaction to this is not recorded, but he can't have been any too pleased.

Several small towns lie close by. Kildare, once the site of artillery headquarters based in McGee barracks, lies just three miles away on the road to the south and west, Kilcullen is situated four miles due west in the direction of Wicklow and the huge military camp in the Glen of Imaal, while Newbridge, home to many serving and ex-soldiers and their families, straddles the main road north to the capital, Dublin.

Miss Elsie Sandes from Tralee, the founder of Sandes Soldiers Homes, famous throughout the world of the British Empire, built her very first establishment on the Curragh, and soon Sandes branches were established in faraway places like Australia, Burma, India and Africa. Additionally, certain traders were given special permission by the British to operate on the Curragh and many cadets remember with affection the little old fruit lady with the ass and cart who plied her trade every pay-day around all the barracks as late as the nineteen sixties.

But besides being the HQ of the army, the Curragh is also the centre of the horse-racing industry in Ireland. Scores of training stables are situated all around, and early every morning hundreds of horses can be seen heading for the gallops at the edge of the plains to get themselves in trim for the battles that lie ahead. People eat, sleep and breathe horses in the Curragh area - you can't go into a shop, pub or garage or even to get your hair cut without someone giving you a tip, a 'dead cert', for a horse due to run shortly.

From the moment we stepped off the train at the railway station in nearby Kildare on a bitterly cold January day, there was hardly time to draw our breath. Issuing kit took a full day's activity - two pairs of green 'bullswool' tunics and slacks, one pair of fatigues, two pairs of boots, five pairs of woolly socks, three vests and underpants, groundsheet, three towels, Lee-Enfield rifle, web belt, bayonet, caps, razor and wobbling brush, white PE sweater, shorts and gym-shoes, belts, buckles and blanco, and a strange assortment of other odds and ends and bits and pieces.

Buttons of all shapes and sizes, spare patches of cloth, needles and thread. Needles and thread? Surely they didn't expect us to..... but it seems that they did! The tailor did the heavy-duty repairs, but everything else, like ripped seams or darning socks, was our own responsibility. Tins of brasso, cardinal red and oxtail polish and an array of brushes meant a veritable whirlwind of polishing and shining, cleaning and darning, patching and mending, with the grim realisation dawning that our days dossing at home with mother were finally over.

The boots were hard, brown, bovver-style monsters, with rows of heavy steel studs weighing them down like ton weights. To soften them up, we'd stand in a hot bath until they were completely soaked, then walk around in them for a couple of hours. Naturally this took a lot of the dye out as well, but liberal applications of oxtail polish vigorously applied with the handle of a toothbrush soon put that to rights.

And the shirts! These were collarless, rough-haired and shapeless, like something you'd expect to see on a medieval monk in a monastery. When you put them on they itched like mad, but eventually we cottoned on to the fact that if you wore them for weeks on end without washing or taking a shower, they seemed to blend in with your skin and soon you didn't even notice them.

Then came reveille at 7am sharp, after a sleepless night spent tossing and turning on a narrow rock-hard bed, then out into the freezing half-light for an early morning run across the frost-white plains towards Donnelly's Hollow a couple of miles away, being loudly slagged off by the jockey-boys on their way to the gallops. Donnelly's Hollow is a sunken area at the edge of the Curragh where in 1815 Dan Donnelly, the famous bare-knuckle Irish pugilist, defeated the English champion, George Cooper, in eleven rounds in front of an enormous crowd. Donnelly's arms were so long he could tie his knee-breeches without bending, and his withered right arm now hangs in the pub which bears his name in nearby Kilcullen.

Back for breakfast, after which the billet was cleaned and the beds made and tidied. This was tricky enough, because the sheets had to be folded in such a way as to show the blue line running through them and had to be checked to see if they ran parallel. Then out on parade for inspection, first by the cadet captain, then by the section corporal, next by the company sergeant, and finally by the class officer. This was usually little more than a formality, but at nine o'clock on the dot the real business of the day began.

The entire day was planned to a T, divided up into classes of threequarters of an hour each - bayonet training, judging distance, unarmed combat and the obstacle course, interspersed with visits to the classroom for lectures on military history, leadership, army regulations, and courtesy and etiquette. All movements to and from classes were performed on the double, there was never any time to relax. Someone was always yelling orders. "Hurry up, fall-in, quick march, double march. Straighten up that fucking line, it's like a dog's piss in the snow!"

And the drilling! The non-stop, interminable drilling! Up and down the square, up and down, over and back, then up and down again. "Left, right, left, right, left ... Clé deas clé deas clé ..." Up and down, over and back. "Left turn, right turn, about turn, pick 'em up there, I said PICK 'EM UP. Clé deas clé deas clé..." Military College NCOs earned extra grade pay for issuing their commands in Irish.

They even trundled on a metronome which, set at the rapid rate of 140 beats to the minute, tick-tocked its monotonous tone while several sections of cadets struggled manfully to keep up with the beat. "Clé deas clé deas clé ...."

On and on it went, commands ringing in our ears without a break. "Fall-in, fall-out, on the double, clé deas clé, order arms, fix bayonets, straighten up, clé deas clé, PE kit, bicycle shed, showers parade, clé deas clé, get a haircut, about turn, on the double, clé deas clé, slow march, mark time, get those knees up, HIGHER I SAID YOU SLOPPY BOLLOCKS, clé deas clé deas clé ...."

The only break was when we finally collapsed into bed late at night, after an evening spent frantically cleaning and polishing - boots, web-belt, brasses, pack, linoleum, bicycle, rifle, bayonet. No more sleeplessness, that rock-hard bed now represented the most luxurious resting place outside the Gresham Hotel. But it seemed no sooner had we closed our eyes than it started all over again.

"Right you lot, on parade, what the hell's keeping you, let's get the show on the road. Form up, WAKE UP, YOU DOPEY FUCKING SHOWER. Fall in, quick march, on the double, clé deas clé deas clé ..." Up and down, over and back, then up and down again. "Clé deas clé deas clé ....."

But crazy as it seemed, there was a purpose to all this frantic bedlam, a carefully-planned system which after only a few short weeks saw the previously disorganised rabble turn into a slick, well-drilled platoon moving briskly across the square at a rapid 140 paces to the minute. Even Smithy, whose coordination was always a bit dodgy, somehow managed to keep in step.

No-one shouted at us now, no need, everyone seemed to know what everyone else was going to do next, to anticipate it and go with it. It was as if all the previously ill-fitting rusty cogs in a giant wheel were suddenly oiled and began to mesh smoothly together in a steady, flowing rhythm.

Two
The B Specials

All this fresh air and exercise gave us appetites like canni-
bals - we were always ravenous. All the cadets dined in one
huge mess-hall, with the various cadet classes occupying separate areas and each section seated at the same table every
time. The meals were served up by privates from the college
company, who were generally sympathetic to the cadets, and
the presence of the orderly officer of the day ensured a modicum of order. Second helpings were an absolute treat whenever we could manage to wheedle them out of the cooks.

The chief cook and bottlewasher was Corporal Cluhatch, a
fearsome scruffy-looking brute with a ready tongue and a vile
turn of phrase who presided over the cookhouse with an iron
fist - even the officers gave him a wide berth. Someone said
he'd been left behind by Napoleon in the retreat from
Moscow, and I can well believe it.

Cluhatch rarely smiled, and it was a brave man indeed who
ventured to criticise his cooking. His penetrating yell of 'No
fucking buckshee!' emanated regularly from the bowels of the
kitchen and was meant to discourage anyone, officers, cadets,
and waiters alike, from looking for second helpings. It soon
became a standard cant. The word 'buckshee' probably comes
from the old Indian army term 'baksheesh', meaning a sort of
handout.

We never found out if Cluhatch was his real name or not, but
somehow it fitted him perfectly, a real Dickensian character in
the mould of Scrooge or Fagin. His most famous riposte was
delivered during an inspection by a visiting catering officer

one day who, having complimented him on the food, innocently enquired if the men had a choice.

"Choice?" he chortled with an evil grin. "Yeah, they've a choice all right. They can fuckin'-well take it or leave it!"

The rate of pay for private soldiers was then six shillings and sixpence a day, and cadets qualified for this lordly sum plus another three and threepence ration allowance, out of which the monthly mess bill had to be paid. While cadets were paid the same as a private soldier, they differed in that they had to pay for their grub. Most of our pay went on supplementing the rations with visits to Maginn's tuck shop just across the road where a tempting variety of biscuits, lemonade, and chocolate was on sale.

You had to be down to meals smartly before all the milk and sugar had disappeared, because that was your lot and no more was available. Whenever the sugar ran out, we'd sometimes put blackcurrant or strawberry jam in our tea just to sweeten it up a bit, even if the colour didn't look any too healthy. As is often customary with people in tough situations, we soon learned to exploit one another's weaknesses, and before long cottoned on to the fact that one of our section, 'Red' Whelan, was equipped with a 'dicky' stomach which invariably let him down whenever any unpleasant subject was broached at the table, resulting in a hasty departure in the direction of the jax.

On the rare occasions when the dessert was particularly inviting, someone would launch into a story with the most vile connotations - guts, gore, lavatory humour or whatever - and pretty soon poor Red would be on his way. Immediately an undignified scramble for possession of his dessert would commence - cruel, perhaps, but the piranha fish shows no mercy. In any case we reasoned that since he was such an outstanding swimmer, we were actually doing him a favour by saving him from eating this type of gooey fattening food, but I'm not too sure if Red saw it that way.

There were three cadet classes in the Military College at the time - the senior cadets, the intermediate class of sixteen known as 'The 16 Dead Men', so-called because of their lazy, laid-back attitude, and my own junior class which numbered forty. Our number eventually swelled to forty-one, caused by a cadet from the 16 Dead Men being sent back for some reason or another.

This wasn't too unusual an occurrence - if a cadet wasn't up to the mark but was deemed worthy of a second chance, or had been sick or injured, then he could be sent back to train for a further year with his junior class. Anything else would ensure he got his 'ticket', i.e. a one-way ticket to civvy street. Not unnaturally, a ticket was a dreaded sentence, one which every cadet did his utmost to avoid. To get your ticket meant failure - failure to keep up to the mark, failure to justify your selection, letting down your instructors, your school, your parents. The shame of it was almost too much to bear.

The senior class was divided in two, the A's and the B's. The nickname for the latter was the 'B Specials', after the infamous Protestant paramilitaries in the North, and we juniors found them a very strange bunch indeed. They kept strictly to themselves, even in the mess hall or at recreation when all classes usually mixed freely, and were unbelievably clannish and supportive of one another. Questions were invariably met with suspicion, hostility even, as if they wished to blank an unpleasant memory from their minds. Only much later did we discover the reason why.

The selection of cadets is strictly on merit, a system the army guards jealously - after all, who wants to be saddled with some duffer who'll land you in deep shit in a tricky situation later on. Dealing with subversives in Portlaoise prison, in the Congo, in Lebanon, on the border or wherever, there can be no room for half-wits.

Every effort is made during the selection process to weed out those who can't 'cut the mustard'. At that time, six officers sat on the cadet interview board, armed with every sort of a report on each prospective candidate whom they'd then interview at length, often twice, before settling on the best qualified. Each officer on the board allotted his marks and all were then totalled, and this final placing could not be altered by anyone, no matter how high up or influential he might be. This was considered the best way to ensure fairness and avoid nepotism which as everyone knows can be endemic if unchecked.

You couldn't get fairer than that - if you were good enough, you were in with a chance, no matter who you were or how humble your family status might be. It was all up to yourself, 'pull' got you nowhere, though this didn't prevent people from trying - the patronage system is deeply ingrained in the Irish psyche. But there's an exception to every rule, and the B Specials were a prime example of how the system can, and did go wrong, with disastrous unforeseen consequences.

The first draft of thirty-nine cadets, the A Class, arrived in the Military College in November 1950, hoping to become commissioned officers. But the last cadet on this list, the 39th, had in fact been placed only 92nd on the original list and had apparently been 'pulled' in at the insistence of a highly-placed politician, whose son he was. Thus he had managed to leap-frog over all those placed higher than himself on the original list.

Everything went smoothly enough for a time, until some meddlesome sort leaked the story to the opposition political party and then the balloon went up and the manure hit the fan. In order to save face and cover up the original blunder, the departmental authorities were left with no option but to call up all those intervening numbers between thirty-nine and ninety-two, and the politicians duly issued the orders to a reluctant army.

So it was that the following May a further 53 cadets received the call to report to the Cadet School in the Military College. In order to distinguish them from the A's, this new class now became designated as the B Class and, being a special enlist-ment, naturally enough they were soon christened the 'B Specials'. Needless to say, the Army was very unhappy with this situation and promptly decided that it wouldn't be dictat-ed to by any shower of politicians, no matter what their posi-tion or influence. The harsh message came whizzing down the army line - get rid of the B Specials, by fair means or foul.

From that time on, they were subjected to a reign of terror unique in the illustrious annals of the Military College. From dawn to dusk they were harried, bullied and pressurised in a determined effort to break their morale and force resignations.

Their inaugural interview in O'Connell lecture hall set the scene - the army didn't want them, a grim-faced Cadet Master told them, they weren't welcome in the cadet school and the army intended to get rid of them by hook or by crook. At first the B-Special cadets were inclined to treat these menacing threats with a certain amount of amusement, mistakenly believing that this was the normal way new recruits were treated, part of the toughening-up process that you see in films like From Here To Eternity. They weren't too long in learning the reality.

Their first visit to the swimming pool almost ended in disaster. Swimming lessons for all new recruits was mandatory and cadets were taught to swim over an extended period, but the B's were left in no doubt that failure to swim a length of the pool in full battle order, complete with rifle and helmet, meant immediately getting their ticket, whereupon several poor swimmers, including some who couldn't swim at all, recklessly hurled themselves into the pool in a desperate attempt to avoid dismissal. It was only when several were hauled out more dead than alive that the experiment was abandoned in case a fatality occurred, in which case providing an explanation could have been very awkward indeed.

Then barely three weeks later, even before their boots and equipment were properly broken in, they were force-marched in full gear - rifle, helmet, ammunition, pack, bedding, and pick and shovel - all the way to the Glen of Imaal for manoeuvres. Normally this wouldn't occur for several months until they were properly hardened up with lots of PE, square-bashing, training runs and so on, but for them there was to be no mercy.

For several weeks the pressure was piled on - route marches, mountain climbs, night patrols, forced marches, and section and platoon attacks, where cadets were tested for their leadership qualities. A full colonel was attached to each section, an unheard-of procedure prior to this, and these were left in no doubt about their brief - weed them out.

And weed them out they did, in a brutal and ruthless manner that failed to take into account the well-being of those misfortunate young men, entirely innocent of any wrong-doing, who were completely unaware of the political power play being enacted above their heads. Pressure was piled on pressure, physical hardship and mental stress became the norm.

At long last, as the end of the first year approached, with the 92 cadets still grimly hanging on for dear life, plans were being made for a big celebration to mark their survival, when suddenly out of the blue a number were summoned to appear before the cadet administrative officer.

Without a word, he handed each of the stunned cadets a plain brown envelope. Inside were their 'tickets'. No excuses, no soft words of apology, no explanations, just a terse note telling them their services were no longer required.

They were to leave immediately, the note said, it wouldn't do to have them hanging around corrupting the others and haunting the place with their failure - or perhaps those in charge were too ashamed to look them straight in the face? By that evening they were gone, just like that. Bye bye baby and thanks a lot.

I often wondered what happened to those young men, the vast majority of them decent fellows who tried to do their best but weren't deemed good enough by their military masters. It may well be that some just weren't good enough, weren't quite up to the mark, but how afterwards did they cope with the undoubted stigma of being dismissed, of being shafted unfairly, of being found wanting in their chosen profession? Did they survive, do well, lose the scars ?

Hopefully they did, but somehow I have my doubts. After a year of turmoil and hardship, of honest effort and shared comradeship, of final rejection and humiliation, how could any young man escape being permanently scarred by an experience which might have been dreamed up in some weird

Kafkaesque horror story. I know that one young fellow was fished out of the canal some years later, but alas no-one ever followed up that story.

For the duration of their final year, the remaining B Specials lived in permanent dread of getting the boot - every time anyone carrying an envelope approached, the whole class quaked in fear. No-one knew when and where the axe would fall next nor what the criterion for success or failure might be. It was a dreadful time to be a cadet.

In due course 34 B Special cadets made the commissioning ceremony, out of the original 53. A total of twenty five cadets got their tickets, 19 from the B Specials and six from the A class. Though many of the survivors eventually went on to become outstanding high-ranking officers, bitter memories of the affair still rankle.

So painful duty was done, and the honour of the army preserved - but at what a dreadful cost? While it's true that many of the Military College staff instructors, officers and NCOs alike, were at a loss to understand what was happening or why and vainly tried to reconcile the principles of decency and honourable behaviour preached in the cadet school with this kind of shabby carry-on, alas there were others who entered into the spirit of the witchhunt with lamentable gusto.

The one man with the courage to make a stand was Capt. Vin Bastin, the famous Waterford hurler, but he duly paid the penalty - he was humiliatingly relieved of command of his cadet class, but at least retained his honour. Thus ended one of the most sordid episodes in the entire history of the Military College.

Three
A Case of Flatulence

My class arrived towards the tail end of this period, to face an atmosphere of resentment and suspicion. Though I suppose he did his duty as he saw it, the Cadet Master had brought the technique of instilling fear to a fine art, holding the power of dismissal in his hands as he did.

Almost every day, a line of cadets could be seen standing stiffly to attention outside his office awaiting their turn for inquisition. They'd be there as we went to lunch, and they'd be still there on our way back. It was a cruel means of instilling discipline. His lectures, such as they were, invariably deteriorated into an inquisition and usually ended in several cadets being doubled from the lecture hall in disgrace.

During one of these lectures, he was rambling on and on about some pernickety quality of military leadership or other, when suddenly he fixed his beady gaze upon a sleepy-looking cadet sitting dozing in the back row. Fixing him with his most intimidating stare, he proceeded to give him a first-degree grilling.

"Fortitude ... And what is fortitude......." - a long pause, eyes first flicking here and then there to soften up the rest of the class - "Cadet MacNiocall?" But MacNiocall, a bright lad who'd anticipated the ploy, had previously consulted his dictionary and had the answer off pat.

Leaping to his feet, he barked out loudly "Tenacity in the face of adversity, sir", then sat down again, looking rather pleased with himself. The Cadet Master seemed taken a bit aback by this outburst and paused for a moment, then quickly regained his composure.

"Sit down, you damn fool," he growled, scowling at the hapless cadet. It didn't pay to be too clever in those days.

His very appearance on the parade ground for inspection was a fearful ordeal. Every cadet would merit a full minute's close scrutiny, every item was carefully checked - boots, brasses, rifle, bayonet, haircut, sling - and woe betide anyone found wanting in any way. The culprit's name would then be taken and he'd be instantly doubled from the square to be dealt with later on, either by a period of CB (confined to barracks), by extra drilling or a fine. Either way it was a black mark on his conduct sheet, with the threat of getting his ticket always hovering in the background.

By the time the inspection team arrived at our platoon, sometimes up to two hours later, we'd be almost frozen to the spot and unable to move when finally called to attention. Every now and then a commotion would signal yet another cadet crashing unconscious to the ground, to be quickly dragged away by the NCOs. On one particular day, the long parallel lines of sweat marks left by the boots of our platoon were clearly visible on the flinty ground as we marched away.

Nor was anyone immune from criticism. One inspection day the Cadet Master dallied in front of me, earnestly seeking a flaw. I was pretty confident my turn-out was faultless, but suddenly he produced a pin from the lapel of his tunic, removed the bolt of my rifle and, after rooting around in a tiny gas aperture for an age, held up the pin in front of my face.

"What's that, cadet?" he enquired, pointing at the head of the pin, cold steely gaze boring into me. I stared blankly, unable to see anything, unless perhaps it was minute specks of iron filings he'd managed to gouge out from the steel.

"That's gravel," he grated. "And if you were in the Korean War, you'd be brought behind the guardroom and a shot would ring out." There was no answering that, so I contented myself with the mutinous thought that if a shot did ring out, it wouldn't be for me!

I suppose it's in the nature of things that people remember the good times, the things that make them laugh, rather than dwelling on the hardships of the past. Every autocratic institution breeds its own moments of light relief, nursing, teaching, the police, or whatever. This is what makes life tolerable; those who wallow in gloom are usually avoided like the plague.

One Saturday morning the three cadet classes and the college company were all lined up on the square awaiting inspection by the Cadet Master, with their officers and NCOs fore and aft. The inspection team moved slowly through the ranks like a snail with arthritis, checking here, finding fault there, names being noted in notebooks for attention later on.

In the background the No. 3 Army Band under Capt. Denis Mellerick was blaring out a medley of Sousa marching tunes, the music echoing eerily back from the surrounding buildings but scarcely appreciated by the ranks of half-frozen men standing there patiently awaiting their fate. After a while the band stopped playing, the silence deepening as the music slowly died away.

Then suddenly, someone let fly a mighty fart which seemed to split the air. In the deep silence it sounded just like an exploding mortar shell, causing people to stiffen in amazed shock. A barely-suppressed titter broke out here and there in the ranks as everyone fought to control their merriment, but if the CO heard anything he certainly gave no indication, continuing urbanely with the inspection as if nothing untoward had happened.

Then from the rear of the class came a loud whinny of laughter which set off a whole chain reaction of muffled guffaws from the ranks of the platoons as the tension dissolved. There could be no mistaking that whinny - it was Sgt. Bill Hartley's trademark. Hartley was a committed, conscientious and extremely able NCO, whose only fault was that he thought the sun shone out of his best mate Sgt. Troy's arse.

Jack Troy was a genial, comfortably-built man with a sly sense of humour and a fund of filthy stories delivered with dead-pan seriousness, which usually reduced his listeners to tears of helpless laughter, but he also had a wonderful capacity for sinking copious pints of Guinness in the NCOs mess on a Friday night, thereby giving rise to bouts of severe flatulence, and it was this that led to his downfall. But while he undoubtedly was the cause of all the trouble, Jack somehow managed to keep a straight face while poor Hartley exploded.

An expectant hush now settled on the parade ground, with everybody quaking in their boots. The fat really was in the fire this time, somebody would definitely get their ticket. All eyes were on the Cadet Master as he paused, then slowly, very slowly, made his way around to the back of the parade until he stood right in front of the unfortunate sergeant, by now aware of his precarious position and no longer laughing.

"Sgt. Hartley," he intoned, in his cold gravelly monotone. "Did you make that noise?"

"Well, sir, I...I...I..." spluttered poor Hartley, wishing he were anywhere else on this earth at that particular moment.

"Get off the square this instant, do you hear me. Get off this square, at the double. I'll deal with you later".

So the poor sergeant was forced to make an ignominious exit from the parade ground, watched by the pensive ranks, Jack Troy among them. There would be hell to pay for this; the Cadet Master in a good mood was bad enough, but in a foul mood like this ....

We never knew what punishment was dished out, but whatever it was it didn't seem to make too much difference to the two sergeants, who remained as thick as thieves afterwards and managed to survive the episode alright, in fact Troy became something of a folk hero as a result. Maybe the Cadet Master had a hidden sense of humour after all.

The annual boxing tournament, one of the sporting highlights of the year, came up at the end of January. This took place in the old gymnasium, a huge barn of a place with rough wooden floors and a corrugated iron roof which was always freezing cold, even on the warmest summer's day. A ring was erected in the middle and rows of chairs stretched all the way to the back of the hall to contain the spectators. In those days there were very little distractions in the camp, so huge crowds always turned up for the contests, including civilians from areas around.

Every unit in the camp was expected to enter a team in the novice events and the cadet school was no exception. Usually cadets volunteered to box just for the bit of crack, but quite a few were shamed or bulldozed into it by our manager, Capt. Watson, just to make up the numbers.

For a few nights beforehand, everyone boxed a few rounds in the drill-hall or pounded the punch-bag, but for the most part our training was haphazard and none of us was anywhere near fit enough to do ourselves justice in the ring.

On the night of the tournament, we were a bundle of nerves as we togged out in the dressing rooms off the main gym. I'm sure that the rest were, like myself, wishing that they'd never volunteered, but by now it was too late to back out because if you did, you'd never live it down. I was boxing cruiser even though I was really only a middle-weight but, as we had plenty of middles, Aidan Watson moved me up a grade, pointing out that though opponents would be heavier and would hit harder, they'd also be much slower. He was right on all counts.

We sat in the dressing room on the hard wooden benches, gloves tightly strapped on and boxing boots laced high up, togged out in the Cadet School blue strip, towels round our necks and clad in worn old white dressing gowns, looking like lambs prepared for the slaughter. Dessie Ringrose was our team coach, and he kept fussing around us non-stop trying to distract our thoughts from the ordeal to come. Of course he knew well what it would be like, having been there himself the previous year and besides, we knew the Cadet Master was sitting ringside and he didn't forgive lack of pluck easily.

From the gym outside came the roar of the crowd as the bouts got under way, then at last our coach came through the door, pointed to our flyweight, Nicky Hegarty, and shouted loudly "right, you're on." Legs like jelly, Nicky headed bravely out the door to the accompaniment of a chorus of good wishes from all sides. We could hear the announcer introducing the boxers, then the bell rang for the first round.

Almost before we knew it, the door burst open and in came Ringrose supporting a groggy-looking Nicky, his legs dragging behind him. The rest of us could only look on in consternation, petrified at the sight. In quick succession a whole procession of cadets went bravely out, like so many Christian gladiators entering the lions' den, and just as quickly they came back in again, blood gouting from their noses or oozing from cuts over their eyes. It was a terrifying spectacle.

First Hegarty, then Tom McGrath, then Paddy Goggin and Willy Phillips returned, followed rapidly by Sean Berry, all counted out in the first or the second round in a mini-bloodbath. And the crowd loved it and lustily roared their approval.

Then it was my turn. Heart pounding wildly, knees knocking together, I climbed into the ring and sat down in my corner, trying to keep my gaze off my opponent, a big bruiser from the GT Depot with a crew-cut and a broken nose, who kept glaring angrily at me as the announcements were being made. Then the bell sounded and the two of us were left alone in the ring except for the referee, little Micky Gray. There was nowhere left to hide.

For the first minute or two we danced around sizing one another up, throwing the odd few ghost punches which either landed on gloves or on thin air, then I accidentally stuck out a straight left which landed flush on his nose and sent a trickle of blood running down his chin. This seemed to enrage him because during the next clinch, he stuck his face close against mine and roared "I'm going to fucking kill you, Cadet."

But after a while spent easily avoiding his wildest punches, I began to feel a bit more confident, thinking to myself - this is a lot easier than I'd imagined. Aware of all my pals watching, I even tried to look a bit like Errol Flynn in the film Gentleman Jim Corbett, doing a little fancy footwork and dancing round and round and even finding time to sneak an odd glance at the crowd to see how they were taking it. This was a mistake.

Slow though he was, my opponent waited till I was in a corner, then let fly a right hay-maker which caught me on the side of the jaw, shooting my gum-shield from my mouth and sending me crashing onto my backside into the corner ropes.

Luckily for me, the bell sounded just then otherwise I shudder to think what might have happened. My opponent, foaming with rage, was being held back from coming after me, which was just as well because just then my brain was in a spin.

I lay on my stool in the corner almost out for the count, head spinning, millions of stars dancing in front of my eyes. I could taste the blood trickling down my throat and manfully tried to focus on my seconds who were fussing all over me. One poured cold water on top of my head and flapped a towel in my face, while Ringer kept yelling encouragement - "You have him now, you have him now, go in and finish him off."

For the life of me I couldn't see what he was so cocky about, seeing as my opponent had already nearly knocked me clean out of the ring, but somehow I didn't feel this was the right time to point this out.

Then the bell sounded for round two, my seat was pulled from under me and we were off again. My opponent immediately rushed from his corner slinging punches from all angles while the crowd roared encouragement, baying for blood - my blood! - but this time I paid attention to the job on hand and tried to remember the lessons I'd been given as a kid by the great Peter Crotty, Dungarvan's Iron Man, who taught me to spar. I got on my bike and back-pedalled furiously around the ring dodging his wild swings, every now and then peppering him with straight lefts, and to my great relief was just ahead on points at the final bell.

While the crowd usually bayed for cadet's blood - if they couldn't have officer's blood, cadet's was the next best thing - nevertheless they weren't slow to appreciate a good bout, and they gave a sporting standing ovation to a cracking bout between two cadets, Jimmy O'Neill and Tim Harrington. This was a ding-dong battle which none of them deserved to lose, but Harrington just shaded it in the end. Then came a heavyweight battle of the dinosaurs, Mick Tallon and Dave O'Regan, while Liam Young also made a winning appearance.

All in all, we came away with quite a few victories which delighted Watson and the Ringer, but nonetheless it was an experience none of us were keen to repeat in a hurry. It's really unfair to put any youngsters into the ring without preparing them properly for this most gruelling of all sports.

At least in other sports you can lie down or take a breather if you get tired, but in the boxing ring there's nowhere to hide, with some bruiser running around after you intent on knocking your block off.

Later on, however, sitting comfortably with a mug of hot tea and currant buns in the canteen, looking like war-wounded with blotches of red mercurochrome and sticking-plaster stuck all over our faces, the banter and crack more than made up for it all. Say what you like, whether you win or whether you lose, it takes some bottle to even consider climbing into a boxing ring.

Four
Toughening Up

But just as I was beginning to find my feet in the army, something happened which confirmed my suspicion that army medics were definitely a bit crazy. Out playing soccer one day, I jumped to head the ball and ran straight smack into a double-fisted thump from our goalie, big Dave O'Regan, which landed me flat on my back in the middle of the pitch, completely out for the count.

Feeling just a little groggy, I marched off to the nearby military hospital for a check-up and there was interviewed by a bored-looking doctor, who promptly dispatched me for an X-ray. After studying the print for what seemed like an age, the radiologist picked up the phone and murmured conspiratorially into it, every now shooting me a worried glance out of the corner of her eye. Suddenly four hefty orderlies rushed in and lifted me gingerly onto a stretcher, then dumped me unceremoniously into a bed in Ward 3.

For a while silence reigned, then suddenly the bed was surrounded by a bevy of concerned-looking doctors and fussy nurses. The doctors busily consulted charts while the nurses kept rattling trays of evil-looking instruments. Like a rag doll, I was pulled and pushed this way and that, one doctor looking into my eyes with a tiny flashlight, another ordering me to follow his finger with my eyes as he brought it zooming in onto the tip of my nose, while yet another banged away at my kneecaps with a rubber hammer. Not wishing to disappoint him, every now and then I'd give my knee the odd twitch, at which he'd give a non-committal grunt.

Next a pair of determined-looking nurses arrived, brandishing a long list of instructions and announced that henceforth, under no circumstances whatsoever was I to get out of bed, not even to go to the toilet. Furthermore, I was strictly forbidden to talk or exert myself in any way and was to lie flat on my back without a pillow. To make things worse, no radio was allowed, no visitors, nothing.

And now they began to erect a phalanx of screens around my bed, shutting me off from eye contact with the other patients. Thick blinds were nailed onto all the windows, plunging the room into funereal semi-darkness. Just then a sombre-looking NCO, nicknamed Sgt. Death, appeared at my bedside and began to take down my particulars, noting it all down on a lengthy chart.

Name, address, date of birth, height, weight, colour of eyes.... on and on it went for an age. Then, fixing me with a gloomy stare, he enquired my next-of-kin. Next-of-kin? What did he want to know my next-of-kin for? "Well, it's a precaution ... in case anything happens." Seeing signs of panic, Sgt Death gave me his best sepulchral grin and smirked "in case you kick the bucket."

By now I was in a right old state. Was it serious, infectious, fatal? Worried relatives kept ringing up wondering what was the matter, but I wasn't allowed to get out of bed to answer the phone. Day after interminable day passed in a dim haze, broken only by visits from medics who all carried out the same tests over and over again. Nurses tip-toed around my bed, fingers to their lips, shooing away fellow-cadets who came to visit and keeping the other patients at arms length. All requests for information were met with a shake of the head and a pursing of the lips. I was completely incommunicado, cut off from the world, adrift in a sea of darkness.

Needless to say my imagination ran riot, imagining every sort of weird scenario known to man. Had I rabies, scabies, even leprosy? Maybe I was even going to die? Could this then mean the end of my days in the army, an inglorious end to a career which had promised so much? Would I get a state funeral? And if so, wouldn't all my schoolpals at home in Abbeyside be really impressed by all that mournful music and the slow march and everything.

But all I could do was lie there in a sort of stupor, the crashing boredom broken only by visits from doctors and the arrival of my meals. Gradually complete ennui set in - I lay there like a zombie, without even thinking. Worse still, my physical state had seriously deteriorated - it seemed the only thing to prevent complete boredom was to sleep non-stop. On, on and on the days dragged, the time hanging heavy on my hands.

After nearly a month of this, twenty-four days to be exact, I managed to pluck up courage and asked the most senior doctor, a kindly sort, what the problem could possibly be. Seated on the side of the bed, he gravely informed me that I had suffered a fractured skull. The X-rays showed a scar about an inch and half long running along the back of my head, he explained, and they daren't allow me move until it had healed up - how long that would take was in the hands of the gods.

Just then my mind flashed back to a childhood incident some years before during a gang war between ourselves and a rival gang from another school, when an opposing youth had flung a jagged piece of slate which crash-landed on the back of my head, splitting open my skull and causing me to have a few stitches put in. Luckily it quickly healed up and I'd forgotten all about it, though of course the scar still remained, and the incident came flooding back into my memory as clear as the day it had happened.

But as soon as the doctor heard this, his attitude changed completely. He stood gazing at me for a few moments before going stomping off out the door, and within minutes my bed was surrounded by a posse of doctors and nurses, all popping questions and glaring at me in a most hostile fashion. They didn't seem very happy with my answers.

Shortly after that two huge nurses arrived and stood menacingly one at either side of my bed. Acting in unison, they grabbed hold of the mattress and unceremoniously turfed me out onto the floor, quickly stripping the sheets and pillowcases to make it ready to receive its next, and no doubt more deserving, occupant. Sgt. Death then arrived brandishing a sheaf of papers and, almost before I realised it, I'd been discharged from the hospital and was on my way back up to the cadet school and the old routine once more.

On my way out the hospital gate, still shaky on my pins after nearly a month spent lying incommunicado on the flat of my back, who should I pass but the doctor who'd originally misdiagnosed me. Tongue firmly in cheek, I decided to ask him what my prospects were for some sick leave.

"Excuse me, doctor," I began, an oleaginous smile on my face. "I was wondering if you'd care to recommend me for some sick leave on account of ....

At this he stopped and fixed me with an icy glare, holding up both hands palms outwards to cut me short.

"Hold it," said he. "Don't say another word." Then he turned on his heels and stalked away down along the hospital corridor, snarling loudly under his breath "Fucking malingerer", as if somehow or other I was to blame for his mis-diagnosis. Sometimes you just can't win.

The highlight of the cadet training year was the visit to Coolmoney Camp in the Glen of Imaal in Wicklow for infantry manoeuvres. The remote terrain of the glen is rough and rugged, bog and scraw-land mainly, with huge mountains towering round on all sides and plantations of pine and fir trees dotted here and there.

A few hardy farmers tend their flocks of sheep in the glen but generally the land is good for nothing else except soldiering, hence the location of the artillery range, opened for firing heavy guns in 1899. The land on which the camp is built was acquired from the earl of Leinster around that time.

The camp itself is a huge sprawl of wooden huts set in a hollow in the middle of the glen, with soggy marshland all around and a fast-flowing river skirting the bottom. It's an ideal place to test a man's strength, courage and stamina and to put his leadership qualities to the test.

But first of all we had to get there, a march of nearly twenty-five miles carrying full kit, a hefty enough load to test even the toughest. Then, immediately on arrival, we dug in and were then launched into an endless round of section and platoon in attack, forced marches, and long night patrols. It was gruelling, exhausting work, and sometimes when attacking a hill and with the 'enemy' pouring down a hail of blank ammunition, we'd be so knackered that when the order came to charge we'd just lie there, unable to get up, completely impervious to the torrent of abuse and threats coming from the instructors.

The emphasis then switched to defence, with one outfit digging-in on a dominating height and the others attacking this position. This entailed having to live in trenches for several days on end to get the authentic flavour of battle conditions, a reminder of what men had to endure for years during the First World War. Trenches were continually widened and strengthened and revetting installed to prevent the sides collapsing, and drainage was then put in to carry away excess water and a covered shelter built to provide a rest area.

Living in trenches had an entire life of its own. It was hard gruelling work, and hunger was a constant presence. The food was ferried from the food trucks to the trenches in containers, and sometimes the rain and mud added an unwelcome flavour which still didn't prevent it being scoffed without delay.

The cadets and NCO instructors were billeted in wooden huts, long parallel lines of them, heated by pot-bellied iron stoves which glowed red-hot and threw out colossal heat, while the officers bedded down in Coolmoney House, the big house at the top of the slope overlooking the area, now sadly due for demolition. Besides having several large airy rooms and a huge downstairs kitchen, the house boasted a small moat and a dark gloomy cellar and had a classical haunted-house look about it. There's even a haunted room, known as Nelly's room, which was always kept locked and was never opened, not even when the need for extra accommodation was pressing.

Rumour had it that Nelly, a young maid in the Hutchinson family employ, was made pregnant by one of the local gentry. He killed her and threw her out of the window and a large dark stain on the floorboards is reputed to be a bloodstain which can never be washed away. Even when new boards are put in, the stain re-appears. Her soul is said by locals to still haunt the room and, as if to prove the point, an army chaplain blessed the room and prayed for the soul of Nelly and her unborn baby in February 1999.

Some years ago, a group of officers were drinking in the bar when the conversation got around to that room and the reason why it's kept locked. Following a dare, two of the more hard-ened warriors, pouring scorn on myths, traditions and old wives tales, volunteered to spend the night in the room and, well fortified with alcohol, entered and locked the door to shouts of encouragement from their mates.

Early next morning they emerged, ashen-faced and shaking, relating tales of how all night the bed was pulled and pushed all over the room and their bedclothes continually yanked off, while they could sense a cold evil presence in the room which petrified them out of their wits. No one ever slept there again after that.

Years after, when myself obliged to occupy the house all alone while on manoeuvres, I still found it hard to shake off that strange eerie feeling. As you lay in bed, mice scurried across the roof-eaves in a continuous staccato stream, making sleep impossible.

To reach the toilet, you had to descend two flights of granite steps in the gloomy half-light to get to the stone-flagged base-ment, a scary business in the dead of night which was only undertaken under dire pressure. So scary in fact, that I always slept with a loaded pistol under my pillow, just in case!

The grub was nothing short of dire. It wasn't that the army didn't buy the best of food - they did, but if the cooks weren't up to the mark, then nothing on earth could prevent them making a total hash of it. The system of selecting the cooks was the problem, which happily has long since been rectified. It went something like this:

The adjutant would summon the sergeant major to inform him that four men were required to undergo a catering course in the Army School of Catering up in McKee Barracks in Dublin, and who was available? Immediately the sgt. major's eyes would light up at the prospect of getting shut of four absolute 'dodos' for a period of six months or so.

"Ah, that's great news. Well sir, there's 97 Sheehan....and 06 Moloney.... and there's that yoke 44 O'Brien - that should get rid of that shower for a while." Soldiers were often identified by the last two digits of their army numbers.

"Good, good, they're three fucking beauties, right enough," the adjutant would chortle, rubbing his hands with glee at this happy prospect. "Put their names down. Now, who else have we?"

"Let me see ... umm ... er ... ah, yes, the very man. That fucking magpie 83 Guilfoyle is due out of detention in a couple of days, great chance to get shut of him as well."

And so four very reluctant and totally unsuited 'magpies' would be dispatched to the School of Catering to undergo an intensive cook's course. The only problem was that they always came back, whereupon they'd proceed to mangle the very best of food - if they could, they'd burn jelly. Fortunately the army has cottoned on to the damage this kind of system caused, and successful candidates are now paid grade pay which ensures a pretty high standard. There are even several choices available, enough to make poor old Cpl. Cluhatch turn in his grave.

But the grub in the Glen was another day's work. Patriotic dried eggs, so-called because they turned a vivid shade of green, white and gold in the pan, were served up lathered in thick grease, accompanied by Widow's Memories - huge brown bangers of sausages - and lumps of black pudding just like ice-hockey pucks, hard and black.

The spuds were mashed up and a huge knob of rancid butter

hurled in on top and stirred into a sticky mess, with lashings of damp salt added for good measure. Watery turnips which even a starving bullock would turn up his nose at followed, and then came the piece-de-resistance, the dessert.

Made from rice boiled in smelly bog water to a soggy sticky off-white texture, a dollop of pale anaemic-looking yellow custard was ladled all over it till the whole thing resembled nothing less than a seagull's shite, and tasted like it as well. Of course we'd protest like mad about the rice to Chalkie White, the cook corporal, but all he'd ever reply, with a great big happy laugh, was "Well, lads, a billion Chinese can't be wrong!"

Mugs of hot 'chaa' followed, made from water boiled over woodsmoke for hours on end. Fistfuls of tea and sugar were then added and vigorously stirred in with the branch of a tree, leaves and all. Holes would then be punched in tins of condensed milk with a bayonet; by rights the condensed milk should have been drained in slowly but that was really asking too much so in went the tins, milk, labels, the lot.

The liquid left a thick brown scum on the inside of the enamel mugs afterwards which only sand could remove. What it did to our insides hardly bears thinking about, but it was hot, it was strong, so down the hatch it went, leaves, flies, ants, labels, the whole damn shebang. Hunger is indeed good sauce.

In fairness, the stews were always a treat, full of vegetables and thick chunks of juicy beef. We'd know when the grub was on its way by the mouth-watering smell wafting down along the lines of trenches. Men would stand there in the dark, noses sniffing the air just like the Bisto Twins on the soup packets, mess tins in hand; then the scramble for more meat and potatoes, trying frantically to stab a juicy chunk with the long bayonet in the pitch dark.

The smell of damp hung everywhere. Rows of wet fatigues, shirts, socks and boots dangled from makeshift lines all over the place, especially during wet weather. Drying sheds were available, but these were usually too crammed to cope with the demand. And needless to say, the instructors took particular pleasure in making sure you waded through the deepest part of the river, the muckiest part of the swamp which of course they knew like the backs of their hands.

Shaving in the early-morning cold was always a problem. The water was never very hot, and as a result razor blades quickly lost their edge and became rusty. You could regularly see people trying to sharpen their blades on the rim of a glass or along the edge of granite rocks as they hacked away.

This didn't always work too well, and they would then hack chunks out of their faces trying to shave. The wounds would be staunched with pieces of newspaper stuck on all over their faces, leading Sgt. Matty Roche to remark to a bloodied warrior on inspection one day - "If I want to read the Independent, cadet, I'll buy the fucking paper myself, thanks very much."

While first-year cadets were housed in billets, second-year senior cadets were allotted a room to each pair and woe betide you if you didn't get on with your room-mate. A most peculiar aspect of all these rooms was that no-one ever placed a foot on the linoleum floors, except the inspecting officers. These floors were kept so highly polished that you just stepped onto lumps of waxed old blankets and then slid your way around, which of course merely added to the overall glow.

The final months of the cadet course were devoted to various aspects of leadership, organisation, and planning. Essays on great military campaigns were handed in and analysed, lectures by eminent personalities were arranged, and debates against outside colleges held.

The lives and careers of the great leaders were assiduously studied and, on one occasion, great excitement was generated by the visit of the famous German dare-devil, Col. Otto Skorzeny, who organised and carried out the daring crash-landing glider rescue of Benito Mussolini from his impregnable mountain prison and was at that time living in Kildare. It was a strange sensation to actually see a real live war-hero standing before us in the flesh.

Visits to the various corps followed, to study their organisation and to assess the assistance they could provide to infantry in battle situations; these included the Air Corps, the Naval Service, Cavalry and Artillery among others.

During our visit to Haulbowline, someone pointed out the two hoary old captains living alone in the officers mess who hadn't spoken to one another in years - they even resorted to ringing the bell to call the waiter every time they wanted the salt or pepper, rather than ask the other to pass them along. The whole thing made you wonder why someone higher up hadn't seen fit to knock their heads together long before this.

Triangular competitions in athletics, gaelic football and rugby, involving ourselves and neighbouring Newbridge and Clongowes Colleges, usually resulted in us running away with the athletics and gaelic, but surprisingly, we were nearly always comprehensively walloped in the rugby despite being much bigger and heavier than our opponents.

Nor were the social graces entirely neglected. Receptions and dress balls were organised, visits to concerts and theatres arranged, and a general appreciation of the finer points of arts and culture imparted.

The final culmination came on the day when the successful cadets were presented with their commissions by the minister for defence on the barrack square and received their first salutes from the sergeant major, in the presence of their admiring families and friends, while the army provided due pomp and ceremony.

Five
The Meadow of Honey

At the end of two long years of very hard graft, I found myself posted to the Southern Command, to the 13th Infantry Battalion stationed in Clonmel. Most of my classmates were sent to infantry units, but a fair few got posted to the units of their choice and departed for the various corps - Cavalry, Artillery, Supply & Transport or Signals, while a handful went to the Air Corps in Baldonnel or to the Naval Service. I had no idea what Clonmel would be like, but it didn't turn out a bit like I'd expected.

The name Clonmel derives from the Irish name Cluain Meala, which literally means The Meadow of Honey. Clonmel is a lovely rural town nestling on the banks of the river Suir, under the shadow of the Comeragh mountains. It's the capital of Tipperary, situated in the very south of the county, right on the borders with Waterford.

All I knew about Tipperary was that they used to win All-Ireland hurling titles with monotonous regularity, usually at the expense of my own county Waterford, but Waterford lay just over the gas-house bridge spanning the river and home was just an hour away on my motorbike.

Clonmel's cheery modern barracks made a welcome change from the dreary red-brick buildings of the Curragh. Situated bang in the middle of the town, it was pleasant to look out of the windows and see the purple mountains towering over the town and to watch civilians hurrying to and fro, a welcome change from the almost-totally army personnel of the Curragh, famous for its three S's - sheep, shite and soldiers.

Right across the road was the greyhound track, and twice a week the sounds of the dogs' excited yelping and punters roaring on their fancies would drift over to the officers mess just

34

inside the main gate. Clonmel is a great sporting town, hunting, racing and fishing country, and is the mecca of greyhound enthusiasts who gather there in their thousands every February for the annual coursing festival.

Clonmel turned out to be a lovely, unpretentious town with a warm, friendly atmosphere and I loved it from the start. It would be impossible not to make friends there, and besides, the place bulged with colourful characters only too willing to share a bit of diversion.

A number of townspeople were members of the officers mess and visited regularly, though this was inclined to depend on whether the CO had a friendly attitude or not, while many officers met their future wives or made life-long friends in the town. I still have fond memories of people like Noel Magnier, Liam Curran, Noel Stapleton, Vincent Fox, Pat Howley, the Dougan brothers, Maurice and Peter, Frank Kent, Eddie Hickey, Willy Treacy, and numerous others.

The town also had a great relationship with the army, and was thankfully devoid of the hostility which still lingers in some areas towards the military, more than likely a hang-over from British days. There's that wonderful air of manliness in Tipperary, a sense of their own identity, their place in history.

The soldiers from the area also typified this attitude - they were Dan Breen's men, independent, fearless, manly. You never felt any resentment in their attitudes, they took you as they found you, but if you were a bit dodgy then they weren't too long about letting you know. They didn't defer to reputations either.

Walking home from athletics training one evening shortly after winning a big competition, with the silvery javelin trailing prominently from my baggage, I passed a few local layabouts in their normal position holding up the wall of the Ritz cinema, busy as usual with solving the world's problems. They stopped as I approached, studying me carefully as they pulled on their cigarettes. Finally one hoary old sweat, fishing flies stuck all over his greasy cap, eyed the javelin with a knowing smirk.

"Catch anything, young lad?" he enquired.

With the arrogance of youth, I naturally assumed he was referring to my recent athletic successes and was more than a little wounded by their roars of laughter when I told them it was a javelin, not a spear, useful only for athletics. As far as they were concerned there was only one use for a thing like that, and that was for stabbing salmon in the nearby Anner river, a practice for which some of them had done a bit of 'time' in the past. It took a while for my ego to recover.

The CO of the barracks was known as Pinky, an egotistical little man with delusions of grandeur who never lost an opportunity of reminding anyone who would listen that he was the successor to a long line of patriot heroes with historical links to the area. He'd obviously been practicing his word of command for ages, because you could hear him roaring miles away as he posed in front of the mirror up in his room.

"Paraaaaid ... AIRE!" he would bawl, drawing out the first syllable for what seemed an age. "De reir clé ... go mear ... mairséal!"

Directly below in the kitchen, the cooks and waiters would take turns to imitate him, strutting around with their bellies sticking out and their arms akimbo. Since Pinky was also small and dumpy, his prancing and preening only made him him look even more ridiculous; he'd stand out in front of the men, crop under his arm like Napoleon, and come out with the most embarrassing roars and bawls.

Pinky then had a further brainwave, which made things even worse. He decided that our drilling coordination could only be improved by seeing our reflections in a mirror, so the following Thursday saw a couple of hundred men standing lined up in rows in the middle of Clonmel's main drag, Gladstone Street, right in front of Woolworth's shop windows. Thursday being a half-day in the town, all the shops closed and drew their blinds and this gave back a reflection.

Pinky stood out in front, chest stuck out like a peacock, bawling out orders like a lunatic while the townspeople looked on in amazement; but while he undoubtedly enjoyed himself, the rest of us nearly died with embarrassment.

Around this time a local young chap called Mally, not quite the full shilling, had taken a shine to the army and haunted the barracks day and night. Though in fact completely harmless, he drove the gate policemen crazy by darting in and out every time they opened up the gates to admit a truck and then defying them to catch him. Mally had an especial love for the pipe band, under the baton of pipe major Sgt. Tom Barrett, and would hang onto the railings fringing the square for hours on end, listening to them practicing and then miming Tom directing the music.

One particular inspection morning, as the pipe band was accompanying the four companies of troops while they went through their intricate drilling on the front square, Pinky arrived to take the inspection. He was all dickied up in his best uniform and could hardly wait to impress the throng of civilians standing watching outside the railings, Mally prominent amongst them.

Just as soon as the band stopped playing, he stepped forward, drew himself up to his full five foot three and, sticking out his chest like a turkey-cock, let out out a prolonged bellow lasting at least ten seconds. The crowd was suitably impressed.

Not Mally! Angry at this interruption to his favourite military music, he suddenly lost patience with this charade and let out an equally impressive bellow. "Hey mister, less of the fuckin' bawlin' and more of the fuckin' music!"

The crowd howled with laughter, delighted at the discomfiture of this pompous little man. Encouraged, Mally launched into a further tirade of abuse directed at the deflated figure fuming with helpless rage, whose thunder he had stolen.

"Get on with the music, you little fat bollocks, or I'll report you to the mayor."

Now the mayor was, if anything, an even bigger omadaun, a doddering old cove long past his sell-by date. Once, while extending a civic welcome to some visitors from Germany, he assured them that, despite the terrible things he'd heard about them and the awful things they had done, he still wished to extend a cead mile failte to Clonmel. Naturally enough, they weren't too impressed.

The crowd responded to Mally's outburst with jeers and cat-calls and, to avoid further embarrassment, the pipe band hastily struck up and the troops marched briskly away, leaving our crestfallen hero to make his way back to the mess in as dignified a manner as possible.

Pinky was never tempted to take a parade on the front square again after that, preferring the less exposed back square to display his powers of delivery rather than risk facing Mally once more. From then on Mally became a hate figure in his eyes, though of course he became highly popular with the locals and the troops.

Clonmel was probably the best school for an innocent straight out of the Military College to learn the ropes. There was quite a lively mess life and lots of good company at all times. There were quite a few hardened drinkers in the place, and rejects from other commands were also packed off to Clonmel as a last staging post prior to getting their tickets. In one year alone, no fewer than thirteen officers faced court-martial for various misdemeanours, which must surely constitute some kind of record for such a small unit.

Many of these people were among the most interesting. I listened open-mouthed in the bar during Christmas while two old drunken captains discussed whether they'd shoot Pinky during dinner or wait until afterwards, but I couldn't be sure if they were serious. The CO couldn't either, because he made damn sure he was never alone in the same place as either of those two ever again. But whatever other qualities these men lacked, courage wasn't one of them - they had their principles, and weren't afraid to stand up for them.

The new CO, Joe Cunningham, was a typical hail-fellow-well-met but he was also miserably mean. He'd entertain guests lavishly in the mess bar, impressing them no end, then slyly write off the bill to mess funds.

One night in Fethard, he met a local artist who'd just completed a painting of the patriot Charles Kickham, after whom

Clonmel barracks is named. He flattered Joe outrageously while plying him generously with drink, and before the night was out had somehow managed to persuade him to purchase the painting for the mess. But in fact the painting was an amateurish mishmash painted on hardboard, the dominant feature of which was Kickham's huge brown overcoat.

Now all that remained was for Joe to convince the mess members, and a meeting was quickly convened to endorse the purchase of the portrait, by now hanging in a place of honour over the ante-room fireplace. The vote was quickly proposed and seconded, which was only to be expected - men of his type are rarely without a clutch of sycophants in tow.

But then to my amazement, the adjutant, a quiet, unassuming man, got to his feet and opposed the motion. It was an appalling painting, Pat Daly announced, and grossly over-priced as well, and he for one had grave reservations concerning the manner of its purchase. You could hear a pin drop when he finished, while Col. Joe's mouth hung open in astonishment. Then Jim McElligott, a dour Kerryman with a reputation for fearlessness, rose and seconded Pat's motion.

When Joe had recovered somewhat, he launched into a harangue about the desirability of acquiring such a fine painting for the mess. Those opposing the motion, he blustered, knew little or nothing about the finer points of art. The vote was duly taken, and the mess secretary announced the result; for, 6 votes - against, 13. Enraged, Joe called for a second vote, but again the result went against him.

At this he completely lost his cool. This kind of behaviour was nothing short of a disgrace, he raged, and he had no intention of standing for it any longer. Those opposing him were insolent and insubordinate, and it was obvious that they harboured a personal grudge against him. He had his own ways of sorting out such awkward people, he blustered, and he would deal with them in his own good time. In the meantime, the meeting would re-convene at 1700 hours, after normal duty hours, and would stay in session until such time as they had come to their senses.

At 17.00 hours on the dot, all available officers assembled in the luxuriously-appointed ante-room, under the baleful glare of the famous patriot who happily remained unaware of the furore his portrait was causing. An unmistakable air of tension hung in the air.

The CO again led off by outlining the desirability of having a memento of Charles Kickham hanging in the barracks which bore his name, and went on to sing the praises of the portrait under discussion. And, he warned ominously, he wanted no more of the scandalous behaviour which had marred that morning's meeting.

The motion to buy the painting was then proposed and seconded, but once again the adjutant arose and put his counter-proposal to the meeting. In his mild manner, he reminded everyone that the mess was democratic, rank couldn't be pulled by anyone, and even the most junior second lieutenant's vote had as much value as that of the highest-ranking general. Furthermore, he reminded the CO, there were limits to his powers in this matter. Again the majority voted for rejecting the sale.

Olly Parker, the mess corporal, was formally instructed to remove the painting from over the fireplace, which he did with great glee. Trusted men such as Olly often took a greater pride in the appearance of the mess than the officers themselves and gladly acted as curators of the mess silver and sundry other treasures.

The painting eventually found a resting place in the mess store amongst all the other bric-a-brac to await its final dispatch back to its creator, but in actual fact it never left the mess at all.

In an underhand action perhaps typical of its originators, the pro-lobby waited till most officers were absent on duty or away on leave, then hurriedly convened a special meeting to reactivate the purchase. This time there were very few to oppose the motion, and the portrait was duly reinstated in its place of honour over the mess fireplace where, as far as I know, it still hangs to this very day.

Six
The Great Kanda

Shortly after that, Jim Shanahan had another of his brilliant brainwaves. He would organise a major concert in the barracks gymnasium in aid of the Army Benevolent Fund, and put on a number of spoof acts which would have them rolling in the aisles.

As usual, his brain ran amok with off-the-wall ideas, and if even half of them had been put into operation we'd all have been run out of town. Anyone who could play any kind of musical instrument was press-ganged into service, while even the most dodgy voice was stuck into a chorus to back up good singers like BFW (barracks foreman of works) Seamus Patterson, a fine baritone, who in the opinion of many good judges had an even better voice than his more famous son Frank.

The term BFW had its other uses. Whenever a whiz-kid young second lieutenant straight out of the college arrived in the unit, brim-full of zeal and intent on reforming the entire army, and started making waves and showing the rest up in a bad light, he'd disparagingly be referred to as the BFW i.e. 'boy fucking wonder!'

Some of the sketches were really ripe. One featured an army medic examining a new recruit (Collins the storeman), attended by an exotic nurse in the form of Sgt. Christy Grogan, clad in a skimpy dress and with false boobs that would make Baywatch look distinctly out of date. Lt. Pat Grennan was in charge of this part of the show and spared no effort in making it raunchy. Fortunately much of the dialogue was censored, but enough remained to make the chaplain and his guests squirm in their seats with embarrassment when the show went out live.

The piece de resistance was the appearance of The Great

Kanda, a magician flown in specially from India for the occasion. Shanahan even arranged for the battalion pipe band to meet him on his arrival at the train station and parade him through the streets of the town as a publicity stunt - all it needed was a couple of elephants to make it look really authentic.

But in truth there was no Kanda at all, simply C/S Mick Sullivan dressed up in a turban and flowing gown, his face painted a deep mahogany for the occasion. He'd been hidden in the boot of a staff car and driven to Limerick Junction station, from where he'd been put on the train for Clonmel. With a few jars under his belt, Sullivan put on a terrific performance, waving imperiously to the crowd and addressing them in the most attractive mumbo-jumbo. Thankfully no-one copped on.

With all the attention our publicity machine was generating, the concert was soon a sell-out, and such was the demand for tickets that it had to be switched to the larger municipal theatre across the road, which in turn was booked solidly within a few days. Clonmel had never seen anything like it, and the hall could have been filled twice over if more space had been available.

Shanahan was delighted. He could see himself in his new role of concert impresario, hiring, firing and fixing at will - but disaster was close at hand. On the night before the concert, Mick Sullivan went on a tear and drank himself into a cocked hat, and by the next morning it was obvious to everyone that there wasn't a hope in hell of him topping the bill as The Great Kanda.

Jim now went into panic mode. All of a sudden his carefully-laid plans looked like crashing down around his ears, with every likelihood of his being banished to Kilworth for the rest of his army career. A deep mood of despondency descended, but not for long. With irrepressible men like him, ideas come tumbling through their minds in an unstoppable torrent. Suddenly his face lit up, and grabbing me by the arm he shouted "I have it, you'll make an ideal Kanda."

Before I knew what was happening, he had it all arranged. I would stand in for Sullivan and put on a whole series of stunts and tricks, all of which would then go spectacularly wrong, in the style of Tommy Cooper. No panic, nothing to worry about at all, just leave it to him and everything would work out just grand. I'd be great, absolutely great, he assured me, and he'd personally make sure I was carefully coached for the occasion. This had to be done, he maintained, I just couldn't leave the side down, now could I? I could, and should, have done, but before I knew it, I had the job.

The night of the concert came and I was in a complete tizzy. Everyone was in the bar tanking up for hours beforehand, and I joined the gang for the first few snifters I had ever had in my whole life. These undoubtedly gave me a degree of Dutch courage - let's go, up and at 'em, let's get the show on the road.

The hall was packed to the doors when the concert commenced, with queues of people begging to be let in. All the brass were there, seated prominently in the front row with their wives, eagerly awaiting the arrival of The Great Kanda.

The preliminary acts were well-received. Pat Grennan's 'chorus girls', complete with fluffy bows on hairy thighs and low-cut false decolletage, preened and pranced on stage making absolute idiots of themselves, to the great delight of their friends in the audience who clapped them to the core. In the front row, however, the brass and invited guests were noticeably lacking in enthusiasm.

Finally my big moment arrived. I should have been a bundle of nerves, but what with regular swigs of from Shanahan's special bottle I was ready for anything. Dressed up in Kanda's exotic eastern outfit, I made my appearance on stage to the sound of mysterious oriental music. Through the haze of alcohol, I could see the serried rows of faces expectantly gazing up at me.

For the next fifteen minutes, I went through carefully rehearsed tricks, breaking eggs into people's hats which then cascaded down round their ears instead of disappearing, pulling pigeons and rabbits out of people's underwear, and a variety of other stunts which all backfired gloriously.

At first the audience didn't know quite what to make of it, but gradually they began to realise that the whole thing was a glorious spoof and soon entered into the swing of things, and by the time the piece de resistance, the sawing-in-half arrived, they were ready for anything.

I don't know exactly how Shanahan arranged it, probably with the help of Tony Lee, the battalion medic, but the idea was that a beautiful young lady (Sheehan the medical orderly, suitably tarted up) would climb into a coffin-like contraption and I would then proceed to saw him/her up. But when the audience heard the terrible screams of the poor victim, and saw the awful gouts of (sheep's) blood pouring down the side of the contraption, they didn't know whether to laugh or to cry.

Out of the corner of my eye I could see the CO sliding deeper and deeper into his plush seat, hiding his face in his hand, which didn't augur too well for the future. At long last the ordeal drew to a close and the bemused audience filed slowly out into the night, wondering if they'd been entertained or completely conned. The jury is still out on that.

Over in the mess bar, the party went on into the small hours. Shanahan was in high glee, insisting that it was the greatest show ever seen in Clonmel and proclaiming his plans for an even bigger extravaganza next year. The Great Kanda, he said, had been an absolute knockout, and he was now considering taking the show on the road to other venues.

The only good thing that could be said about the whole thing was that it brought in one of the greatest amounts of money in the history of the ABF, and also provided a bellyful of laughs into the bargain. For my part, it was my debut and swansong all rolled up into one and, having lain low for a couple of months, I put all thoughts of a show-biz career firmly out of my mind.

There never was a repeat show the next year, or any other year after that either. The general opinion was that we could consider ourselves lucky we weren't all arrested and run out of town, and I thought twice about listening to any more of Jim Shanahan's crazy schemes in a hurry after that.

The 13th Infantry Battalion was fully up to its peacetime strength, in contrast to most of the other battalions in the army at the time. Clonmel had no difficulty attracting recruits not just from Tipperary itself, but also from the surrounding counties of Waterford, Wexford, and Kilkenny.

Most of these were fine, decent, country lads, mostly from farming stock, and they made excellent soldiers. Gone are the days when local police and magistrates got rid of their naughty boys by encouraging them to join the army - nowadays every recruit has to be vouched for by his local garda sergeant, who must then sign a document testifying that his protege has no criminal record.

Each infantry battalion consists of six companies, one of which, HQ, deals almost exclusively with administration - quartermastering, cooking, discipline, transport and the like, though of course all its personnel are armed and expected to be able to shoot and fight as well. Then there is the weapons company, which comprises a number of platoons equipped with various infantry weapons - the heavy machine-gun platoon, the anti-tank, the mortar, and the pioneer assault platoon which deals with mine-laying, explosives, river-crossing and the like. The remaining four companies are infantry only, and are the main fighting force of the battalion. Each company has its own transport, jeeps and such, but the majority of the vehicles are held in the transport pool, to be dispensed as the battalion commander decides.

A fully-equipped infantry brigade in wartime comprises three battalions, and has an immense amount of vehicles under its control, over 700 in all. Include HQ and attachments of artillery and cavalry, and this gives some idea of the problems of control and training involved in getting a unit like that on the move.

All these guns and vehicles have to have fully-trained men to operate them, which entails constant training courses to replace drivers or gunners who leave the army. For instance, it takes almost six months before a machine-gun or mortar crew is fully trained to operate their weapons efficiently as a team. Thus the daily routine behind the walls of a barracks is mainly taken up with training - training recruits, gunners, drivers, cooks, snipers, even administrative staff.

Garrisons like Clonmel simply don't have the space or facilities for adequate training in most of these areas, so places like Kilworth are used for shooting practice and firing heavy weapons. Kilcoran, just beyond Cahir, is a beautiful little range cut right into the middle of scenic mountainside pinewoods but is used for small-arms only, the only danger being deer which occasionally wander across. All firing immediately ceases while they pass.

It's mandatory for every infantryman, from the commanding officer down to the lowliest private, to fire his rifle practices on the open ranges every single year, while some officers specialise in light machine-gun, sniper, pistol and sub-machine gun as well. Artillery and heavy mortars, of course, have to go to the Glen of Imaal for their firing practices, as do the tanks and armoured cars of the cavalry, while most of the serious business of explosives is also carried out in the vast spaces of the Wicklow mountains.

The annual all-army shooting competitions are held in the Curragh every summer; this is the highlight of the Army's calendar, the acid test of a soldier's proficiency in his weapons - to win an All-Army shooting medal is considered one of the most coveted awards. Anyone winning an individual championship is treated like a god and is entitled to wear the marksman's badge on his sleeve for the rest of his army service.

Great rivalry existed in the various units between the top crackshots, especially the riflemen. As the competition season approached, these aces would virtually go into seclusion, behaving like prima donnas and issuing conflicting reports as to their loss of form in the hope of confusing their opponents.

Clonmel's champion, Sgt. Christy Grogan, a colourful character as well as a brilliant shot, would spread the rumour that he'd gone to blazes since his last win and was drinking like a fish, with absolutely no chance of winning, then of course up he'd duly pop on the day of the competition and do the business, collecting some sizeable bets in the process.

I was lucky to have some very fine officers as my company commanders, among them Jim McElligott and Jack Stewart who fearlessly shielded us from Pinky's worst excesses, as did chaplain Fr. John Morrissey from Dungarvan, just returned from hard years spent on the mission in the Australian outback. Pinky did indeed try to throw a saddle on Fr. John as well, but found him more than a match.

Capt. Jim Shanahan from Borris-Ileigh, who later commanded my own outfit, C Company, was a large, swash-buckling Tipperary man with a cheerful outlook on life and the courage of a lion, and the men simply idolised him. He played full-forward on the battalion hurling team, even though he was several stones overweight and carried a prominent beer-belly, but opposing teams quickly learned that this odd-looking, wise-cracking character in ankle socks and baggy togs could both take it and dish it out, and could also hurl a bit as well.

This aroused a certain amount of envy in the CO, whose own leadership qualities could be said to be limited to leading hungry men into the cookhouse. Since he didn't dare tackle Shanahan head-on, the only way he could get back at him was to punish his troops whenever he could in a variety of petty ways. He had to be careful, though, because Jim was a tough man who had established his reputation during the war when coming through the ranks to earn a commission.

About the only way this persecution could be carried out was during inspection, when he'd pick on every possible fault in Shanahan's men, real or imaginary. Needless to say, this caused great resentment among the troops, who genuinely did their best and knew that this criticism was unjustified.

Every afternoon, seven men turned out for inspection as part of the guard, even though only six were actually needed. It was traditional for the best turned-out private, the most 'gildy' man, to be excused duty; this privilege was known as the Stickman and was fiercely contested.

One day the two gildiest man in the entire barracks happened to be on duty at the same time, and there was great anticipation to see which of them, Pte. 'Clawhammer' Doyle or Pte. 'Fuckall' Kelly, would get to be Stickman.

No effort was spared on their preparation. They would spend hours on end cleaning, polishing, and shining their kit, ensuring knife-sharp trouser creases and glittering buttons and brasses. A pair of boots would be specially set aside and never worn except on parade; these would then be boned with the handle of a toothbrush, using Cardinal Red polish, till you could practically see yourself in the toecaps.

The sergeant of the guard and his seven men were drawn up on the square ready for inspection, with dozens of men idly watching from the billet windows or lining the edge of the square, awaiting the arrival of the CO. He moved slowly along the line inspecting the guard, pausing a little longer in front of Clawhammer and Fuckall, who were both absolutely flawless and clearly ahead of the remainder.

But then, to everyone's consternation, he awarded the title of Stickman to another private who, while good, was obviously not in the same league as the other pair. After an embarrassed pause, the winner saluted and moved off, leaving the rest of the guard to march away in the direction of the guardroom, while the spectators looked on in disbelief.

Nothing happened until the following pay-night, when a mighty piss-up ended with the Military Police (PAs) being called to quell a heated argument in the men's canteen over who should have got the Stickman. The argument quickly turned into a near riot, after which most of the men headed out town to continue the discussion in the Slievenamon Bar or Larry Tobin's pub, and an uneasy peace descended on the barracks - for the moment.

An incident like that of the Stickman was not something that could easily be forgiven. All criticisms were taken seriously, especially ones reflecting on the men's professionalism, but when that criticism was blatantly unjust, it quickly became an explosive issue.

Next morning, early risers were startled to find the front square completely littered with debris - rocks, bottles, flowers, shrubs, and tons of earth and rubble, the contents of the newly-erected flower beds which were Pinky's pride and joy.

It was quite clearly a revenge operation. Pinky was beside himself with rage and quickly put pressure on the PAs to find the culprits, and fast. Naturally enough, suspicion promptly focussed on Clawhammer, but he was quickly eliminated from the picture as he'd been at home in bed in Ard-na-Greine.

Fuckall Kelly wasn't quite so lucky. A trail of muddy footprints, plants and creepers led the PAs to his billet, and there they found him lying on his bunk, still out for the count, framed in a halo of daffodils, hyacinths, wallflowers and empty cider bottles, his boots thickly caked in peat moss. No need to look any further.

Poor Kelly, like the Wild Colonial Boy before him, duly departed for Cork to do twenty-one days in the Glasshouse, but his reputation didn't suffer as a result - this was one occasion when the crime was considered well worth the punishment. On his release, Jim Shanahan welcomed him back to C Company with open arms.

Jim had a wonderful way with men, knew how to get the best out of them, though not everyone is blessed with this ability. But his troops knew that he cared, and they would willingly have gone through hell and fire for him. It was perhaps fitting that Shanahan was killed piloting his own plane while managing a mine up in Canada, just like Denys-Finch in the film Out of Africa. Somehow it didn't seem right that a good man like him should just slowly fade away.

Seven
The Bugler Blows Reveille

Kilworth Camp is an army training camp situated on a flat exposed strip of boggy land high up between Fermoy and Mitchelstown, containing several shooting ranges and a grenade-throwing area. Besides its role as a training area for regular troops from the Southern Command, it is also a favourite spot for FCA personnel on weekend training.

Even in summer it can be a bleak and unwelcoming spot, covered with furze bushes and stunted trees cowering sideways away from the merciless wind. The only entertainment is provided by the Blue Dragon pub about a mile away on the road to Fermoy or the nearby Glockamorra Inn.

At long last, after years of waiting, the army decided that Kilworth urgently needed a new officers mess, and a detachment of engineers was sent out from Cork to get it built as quickly as possible. The only problem was to find anyone willing to volunteer for duty there - being sent to Kilworth was like being banished to Siberia.

This problem was solved by the unit adjutants dispatching whichever officers happened to be in bad odour in their units at that time. If you crossed anyone in authority and were in the 'manure business' in your unit, you were quite likely to find yourself heading for a stint in Kilworth.

We were all in the soup together. The CO of the camp had been 'sent down' in disgrace for entertaining a civilian con-man at the Christmas dinner in Galway during the infamous Sir Patrick Murphy' affair. The adjutant, a legendary Cork footballer, had incurred official displeasure by insisting on singing in the mess bar while the local brass tried to play bridge, while the captain had taken a day's uncertified sick leave, a practice greatly frowned upon, after his native Kerry had won the All-Ireland football title the previous Sunday.

My own misdemeanour lay in forgetting to lodge the NCO's mess takings on the last day of the month according to regulations which, while not a heinous crime, was enough under the circumstances to justify being sent to Siberia. So it was that I joined this motley crew in windswept Kilworth with a sinking heart, hoping for the best but expecting the worst, but to my great delight, everyone there turned out to be a wonderful character and not a bit put out by being part of the reject chain-gang.

Almost every night, the bar was crammed with invited locals, swelled by additions from nearby Fermoy and Mitchelstown, and tremendous sing-songs under Eamon Young's baton rang out over the uninviting flat plains. Word spread rapidly throughout the area about the mighty crack going on up in the camp, but if it did, word also spread to HQ in Cork that the lads out in Kilworth, far from being cowed, were having a ball, and this wasn't good enough at all. After all, Kilworth was supposed to be a sort of punishment post, not Butlins - a stop would have to be put to it, and smartly at that.

The choice fell on the 'Tracker' Doyle, a thick-set commandant with jam-jar glasses and shaven bullet-head, totally devoid of any sense of humour, who could be relied upon to put a damper on any festivities. He arrived in Kilworth full of zeal, determined to stamp his baleful authority on the camp without delay.

Since the only troops present in Kilworth were the engineers and the staff, naturally enough discipline was somewhat lax; no great need for spit and polish, no need to swing salutes or any of that nonsense, no-one stood on their dignity, and nobody, but nobody dared to rouse any officer till the square was well and truly aired, which was usually sometime around coffee time.

Every officer had to take turns on orderly officer duty, which included raising the flag at 0730 hours over the main gate, while the remainder lolled in their beds till at least eleven,

even later if they felt the need. As for food, most late-risers made do with what's known in the army as a 'crane's breakfast', i.e. a drink of water and a shite.

My turn to hoist the flag came one cold wet Saturday morning, after a hard session spent in the mess the night before. The sergeant was waiting at the gate with a sleepy-looking guard of six men as I arrived, only to discover to my horror that the Tracker had been there for at least fifteen minutes before me, impatiently looking at his watch.

Just as I was about to raise the flag, he marched across and demanded to know where the bugler was. Now we hadn't laid eyes on 'Puff' Prendergast since the day we arrived, except in the Glockamorra Inn sinking pints - he had a crush on the barmaid and always volunteered for duty in Kilworth whenever he possibly could. A painful period now ensued while Puff was roused from his stupor and hauled on parade, blinking his red-rimmed eyes like a goat in a snow-storm.

"Bugler, sound reveille," commanded the Tracker. Nothing happened. Puff looked at me helplessly, then whispered "Sorry, sir, I can't."

"Why not?" I enquired, sweating under the collar as I felt the Tracker's eyes boring into me.

Silently he pulled an object from his pocket and held it out - it was the mouthpiece of his bugle, completely twisted and flattened due to something heavy falling on it. Reveille this morning was most definitely out of the question.

Not to the Tracker it wasn't! My explanations fell on deaf ears, the bugler's outraged protests cut no ice, the Tracker wanted to hear no excuses whatsoever.

"Get on with it, bugler," he ordered. "That's an order. Blow reveille - or else."

So up we all lined in front of the flagpole once again, the sergeant, the guard, the bugler and myself, presided over by the grim figure of the Tracker. I called the guard to attention and saluted, the sergeant slowly hoisted the tricolour, and the bugler put the bugle to his lips and blew.

Oh, the sound that came out! It sounded like nothing on

earth, like a banshee blowing through the handlebars of a bicycle, a sort of moaning, lowing sound like a sick bullock in a faraway field, complete with terrible puffs and snorts of all descriptions.

There we all stood, rigidly to attention, saluting the flag as it slowly reached the top of the flagpole, to the accompaniment of the strangled sounds of a banjaxed bugle. It was like a scene from a Laurel and Hardy film, except that script would at least have been funny. The word afterwards was that the bugler took to the bottle in a big way, and who could have blamed him - how anyone could ever take the game seriously again after that is beyond me.

I know I didn't.

Every Easter Monday, a huge military parade took place in all the principal cities to mark the Easter Rising which led to the foundation of the state. For the Cork parade, troops from all over the south would assemble in Collins Barracks from as far away as Limerick, Clonmel, Fermoy and Ballincollig, as well as contingents of FCA to help swell the numbers.

For weeks beforehand, frenzied preparations would commence to have men and equipment ship-shape for the march through Cork City on Easter Monday. Intense drilling would take place to smarten up aspects which might have become a little rusty, while vehicles and equipment underwent a complete overhaul and perhaps a lick or two of paint here and there.

Needless to say, preparations in Clonmel never passed without the usual rows breaking out. One of these involved Sgt. Major Joe Browne, who had just been selected to represent Ireland in an international fencing tournament in Edinburgh over the Easter weekend, his first ever Irish cap. This was a great honour and everyone was justly proud of him, but when he applied for leave to attend, Pinky refused his request.

There are, no doubt, those who will argue that everyone, no matter what rank, should be compelled to attend important parades like that in Cork, but when people wonder how mutinies occur, they have only to look at vindictive decisions of this nature. The only possible reason for the refusal was petty jealousy on the CO's part, a case of 'pig-iron', pure and simple; the other row was more amusing.

Larry Fennessey, our quartermaster sergeant, was a roaring dyed-in-the-wool Blueshirt to whom the very thought of saluting Taoiseach Eamon De Valera on the reviewing stand was more than he could stomach. His urgent request to absent himself from the parade was also refused, so Larry had to content himself with turning his eyes to the right, away from the reviewing stand, when the order "Eyes Left" was given.

Every Good Friday, all the troops would come together at noon on the vast barracks square to rehearse the various drill movements in unison. The rest of the time would be spent cleaning and polishing, blancoing and ironing, before assembling once more at three o'clock for the march to the local garrison church to attend the Good Friday religious ceremonies.

It was normally compulsory for all officers to attend parades unless excused, but this parade was the one exception. By tradition, the hardened drinkers would congregate early on in the officer's mess bar to renew old acquaintances and swap reminiscences, while the church parade would be allotted to one of the junior lieutenants just out of the Military College.

Since I was the most junior lieutenant in the 13th, there was no choice but to take charge of the Clonmel contingent, so together with the rest of the units, off we marched at three o'clock to the garrison church at the lower side of the barracks.

The chaplain, Fr. Hugh, was a strict martinet of the old school, a stern, unbending, fire-and-brimstone figure who always took his meals in the mess at the top table with the brass and barely acknowledged anyone below the rank of colonel. And woe betide anyone who dared leave the dining-room before he said grace after meals which, no matter what the hurry of others, he always said in his own good time.

Fr. Hugh took all these parades and ceremonies very seriously, and was inclined to get a bit upset if everyone else didn't do likewise. He was also a great believer in the merits of stern discipline and was convinced that making people toe the line was good for the soul. 'Spare the rod and spoil the child' was a motto he most definitely identified with.

The garrison church was packed to capacity as he mounted the altar for the Good Friday ceremonies and faced the serried rows of men, sitting there solemnly in their pews. After extending a brief welcome, he invited the congregation to join with him in singing a hymn of praise.

"Nearer my God to Thee,
  Nearer to Thee,"

sang the congregation with rapt devotion, Fr. Hugh's deep bass prominent among them.

The sound of hundreds of men's voices raised in song was indeed stirring, warming the very cockles of his heart, but just then, during a pause, the faint sound of other men's voices raised in song came floating dimly through the stained-glass windows from the direction of the officers mess bar a couple of hundred yards away.

"Where I sported and played,
 'Neath its green leafy shade,
  On de banks of my own lovely Leeeee ..."

A slight frown of irritation appeared on Fr. Hugh's brow but, undaunted, he launched into a powerful sermon about the evils of sin and the powers of redemption. He was soon in full flow, completely dominating his captive audience but then, just as he paused for breath, a further blast of a well-known Cork rebel song came drifting in the windows.

"On the twenty eighth day of November,
  The day that the Tans left Macroom ..."

The scowl on Fr. Hugh's face put a stop to the outburst of titters among the congregation. Not to be outdone, he launched into a rousing chorus of Faith of Our Fathers, waving his arms vigorously to encourage everyone to join in. If you can't beat 'em, he reasoned, join 'em!

"Oh, how our hearts beat high with joy-oy,
  Whene'er we hear that glorious word ..."

In the background, the thunderous sound of half-drunken men singing their hearts out ...

"They were loaded in six Crossley tenders,
  As onward they sped to their doom."

The church choir stepped up an octave, their red-faced conductor waving his arms about ever more wildly in a vain attempt to drown out the opposition -

"Faith of our fathers Holy Faith,
  We will be true to Thee till death,
  We wiiillll ..... be true to Deetledet ..."

Over in the mess bar, the rebel song also reached a climax -

"But the boys of Kilmichael were waiting,
  Their shotguns were loaded with shot ...."
And the Irish Republican Armeeeee ...
Made shite of the whole fucking lot."

At this, loud guffaws broke out here and there among the congregation, the men's heads bowed as they struggled manfully to keep a straight face. This was too much for Fr. Hugh. Imparting a hasty blessing, he tore off the altar and headed for the mess bar at a rapid rate of knots, intent on putting a stop to this blasphemous caper without delay.

But when he got there, he found he was unable even to get in the door, the place was so jam-packed. To add insult to injury, Jack Talbot, the self-styled Black Eagle, who'd been leading the chorus with Eamon Young, even had the audacity to ask him if he'd fancy a pint. Incensed, he headed for the GOC's residence a short distance away, where his rage and frustration found a sympathetic ear. However, it was too late to do anything about the irreverent counter-show at that stage, and anyway those in the bar were gone far beyond being intimidated by anyone, let alone the chaplain.

Fr. Hugh had the last laugh, however. He succeeded in closing the bar that evening and kept it closed for the remainder of the weekend, and it never ever opened on a Good Friday again after that.

Collins Barracks lies perched high on top of a hill overlooking Cork City, providing a magnificent grandstand view of the events unfolding below. The old military planners certainly had their wits about them when they selected that particular spot to build their barracks.

The barracks square must surely be one of the biggest anywhere in the world, surrounded as it is on all sides by long grey four-story blocks, grim and forbidding. On one side looms 4th Battalion and Brigade HQ, to the other lies the warren-like mass of single officers quarters, linked by dark and gloomy corridors.

At the far end, the clock tower hangs over an archway dissecting a seemingly endless sweep of classrooms, offices and storerooms, while the end nearest the main gate is dominated by the twin squat buildings of the officers mess. A massive flag-pole flying the huge tricolour is situated half-way between the two messes, with the saluting podium right behind.

Even though Collins Dublin is far older than Collins Cork, the capital's ancient limestone buildings seem to possess a quaint medieval beauty which is somehow lacking in Cork. McKee too has an unique oriental ambience all its own, while even the Curragh Camp projects an imposing domineering essence, especially in summer when the greenness of the trees and shrubbery contrasts pleasantly with the deep red-brick buildings.

Cork is a lovely station, located in a beautiful city, and it ought to have been one of the happiest places to serve in the entire army - but it wasn't. Perhaps it was the sheer grimness of the surroundings or the harshness of the routine, I don't quite know what; but it was there all the same, that strange lurking feeling of menace, you never got that easy relaxed atmosphere that applies in stations elsewhere.

There is this irritating smugness about Cork people which outsiders find very hard to understand, summed up best by the Film Festival which, in their own eyes at least, makes Cork the cultural capital of the world for two weeks. Every army person appreciates the possibility, indeed the probability, of being posted to another unit during their army career, which entails uprooting family and settling in another location, it's one of the hazards of the job which most people learn to accept with as much grace as possible.

Not so in Cork. They'll go to extreme lengths to avoid moving, to the extent of bowing and scraping to an embarrassing degree, which often leads to a craven servility among otherwise manly fellows, an obsequiousness rarely witnessed anywhere else.

This in turn leads to authoritarian attitudes, making for uneasy relationships between senior and junior ranks. Even when posted to another barracks they rarely settle but spend most of their time scheming and plotting to get back to their beloved Cork, watching promotion lists like hawks and submitting transfer applications at every available opportunity.

Another thing that amazed me about Collins Barracks Cork was how so many people found the time to keep their eyes focussed on what was happening out on the square - it was as if it drew their eyes like a magnet.

If perchance you stopped for a moment to have a quick word with a passer-by while on a training period or, God forbid, casually put your hand in your pocket, you could practically guarantee that a PE (please explain) slip would be waiting on your desk on your arrival back into the company office. No wonder Cork became known as The Valley of the Squinting Windows, after the Brinsley McNamara novel.

But while most other messes did their best to avoid any rigorous division according to rank, Cork still managed to observe time-honoured hierarchical dining customs. Fr. Hugh and the GOC insisted on keeping solitary vigils at the top table, being joined by VIPs only on state occasions, while the colonels and commandants occupied the adjoining tables, with the captains and lieutenants left to share the remaining tables as best they could.

Service, too, was on a strict seniority basis. Dan, the crusty old major domo, confined himself to serving the top table only, with the remainder left to depend on the tender mercies of Jimmy and the army waiters. Conversation was generally rather muted, everybody being painfully aware of the baleful presence at the top table.

The only bit of ribald crack came from table three, where Johnny Stapleton regularly entertained fellow-raconteurs Kieran Bradley, Eamon Young, Ted Russell and a few other like-minded bon viveurs.

Johnny, a highly-intelligent man with a biting wit and a rich Tipperary accent, had a raucous voice which was inclined to carry, much to everyone's amusement, including the fossils at the top table who secretly enjoyed him as much as anyone. He would sit there discoursing knowledgeably on every subject under the sun, his trenchant opinions causing ripples of laughter to spread to all corners of the room.

The bane of his life was the command ordnance officer, nicknamed 'the trained seal' because of his extraordinary shape and awkward gait, a complete bore who continually contrived to join Johnny's table despite his best efforts to prevent it. There, once ensconced, he would do his level best to interrupt and score points off Johnny, out of sheer jealousy.

This particular day, Johnny was in full flow on one of his favourite subjects - women, their foibles and their fancies -

when the 'seal' interrupted for the umpteenth time with a question which threw him a bit off balance.

"Tell me, Johnny," the 'seal' began, with a sly smirk. "Is it true what all the women say?"

"And what's that?" enquired Johnny, impatiently.

"They say you have the biggest weapon in the army."

Quick as a flash came the crushing riposte. "Tommy," Johnny replied. "Your wife talks too much."

The room rocked to a roar of delighted laughter, while Fr. Hugh nearly swallowed his soup spoon, but quickly recovered and pretended he had merely choked on a crumb and hadn't really heard a thing.

Eight
Back to the Plains

Feeling a bit frustrated at my lack of academic progress in Clonmel, I now decided to apply for a transfer to either Dublin or Cork in the forlorn hope of attending university classes at night. There was also the added advantage of getting in some badly-needed competition to revive my athletics career which I felt had fallen into a bit of a rut.

In these more enlightened days such a request would be welcomed, even encouraged, but back then it stirred up a real hornet's nest. First my CO gave me a right old dressing-down, reminding me that my army career should be my first and only concern, before announcing with ill-concealed glee that, far from going to Cork or Dublin, he'd arranged for me to be sent to the 3rd Battalion on the Curragh instead.

And so it was that I found myself on my way back to the plains of Kildare once more, a place I'd fervently hoped on my departure for Clonmel that I'd never set eyes on again. It was just typical of the army to send you exactly where you didn't want to go, just out of pig-iron.

It happened so suddenly that I didn't even have time to grasp the reality. One moment I was arriving back from my holidays in Morocco, all sleek and tanned, the next I was in the back of a saloon heading for the plains of Kildare, my holiday bags still unpacked.

I didn't even get time to say goodbye to anyone, to break the news to any of my friends out town. No time to have a farewell drink with my fellow officers, to bid adieu to my orderly, to say goodbye to some of the NCOs and men to whom I had become quite attached. Cheerio, baby, and thanks a lot. See you sometime.

I well remember the awful sinking feeling in the pit of my

stomach as we drove along the banks of the river Suir on our way out of Clonmel, the soft blue Comeraghs on my right seeming to glower in keeping with my mood. On the left Sliabh na mBan had never seemed so beautiful - I gazed at it longingly until it faded from my sight.

I'd never been in Connolly Barracks before, though I'd heard a lot about the legendary 'Bloods' and of course had sometimes come up against them in various sporting and shooting competitions. They were invariably a hardy and determined bunch, with very high morale and a great pride in their unit.

The Curragh has seven barracks in all, each named after one of the seven signatories of the 1916 proclamation. The 3rd Battalion barracks commemorates James Connolly, the others being Plunkett, Ceannt, Clarke, McDermott, McDonagh and Pearse. Most of the Bloods' personnel hailed from Waterford where the unit was stationed during the war, and this to some extent helped me to feel more at home even if the majority were city men, with very few hailing from the west of the county where I came from.

But nothing could have prepared me for the culture shock of their officers mess. Clonmel's fairly modern building is comfortable and welcoming, with a homely warmth and friendliness which quickly puts you at your ease: Connolly was a different kettle of fish altogether. The gardens were indeed imposing, with lots of shrubs and trees and a couple of concrete tennis courts to the right of a sunken garden. The main doors in the middle of the massive red brick building bore the impressive motto 'A Droit de Seigneur' superimposed in the stained-glass centre-piece.

Inside was a very different story. Long, gloomy corridors stretched away endlessly in all directions, dimly lit by low-watt bulbs set high up in the ceilings. Even by day this sense of gloom persisted, helped no doubt by the heavy canopy of trees which blocked out the sunlight on all sides. The walls were tri-coloured; brown, dark brown, and shite-brown, the result, rumour had it, of a Maxie McLoughlin brainstorm -

Maxie was the mess secretary, born and bred on the Curragh, which probably goes a long way to explain the morbid appearance of the place.

The place stank of damp. Large wet patches appeared here and there on the high ceilings; long streaks of moisture ran down the walls and gathered in pools at the base, sometimes running across the marble floor to form great puddles in the middle.

Our bedrooms were enormous affairs, great big ball-alleys almost impossible to heat. The orderlies tried valiantly, lighting turf fires to keep the cold and damp at bay, but the struggle was hopeless.

My room, so rumour had it, was the one allotted to the Prince of Wales on his visit to the then Beresford Barracks to hunt in the early part of the century; he is said to have ravished a local young lovely there, ushered in to provide comfort and company for HRH for the duration of his stay, but alas, things had definitely gone a bit downhill since then, and ushering in any young lovely now meant getting your ticket in a hurry.

The only bright feature was the ante-room. Comfortable lounge chairs and a deep red carpet exuded the impression of opulence. The main feature, however, was the huge red-brick fireplace, over which the flags and emblems of the 3rd Battalion held pride of place. Truckloads of turf and logs ensured a constant roaring fire in the hearth, and this led to people literally toasting themselves in front of the fire every night before finally heading off to the cold comfort of their rooms.

Micheal McGreal, my former room-mate in the cadet school, a roaring nationalist who later became a prominent Jesuit, used to wait up every night to switch off the TV so that the rest of us wouldn't hear God Save The Queen being played at close of programmes on the BBC. You'd have to wonder about that.

Sad at heart, I wandered around the long empty corridors in search of company, but none was to be found. With a heavy heart, I tried to compose myself to sleep, but pleasant visions of Clonmel kept seeping through, plunging me even deeper into gloom. Sleep came late that night.

The rooms were certainly not en suite. You had to toddle off along a shiny linoleum corridor and down a flight of stone steps before reaching the elementary toilets and showers, and I suspect very little has changed since then. I was on my way back from the toilet later on in the night, still half-asleep, when I suddenly became aware of a strange sound in the background.

I paused, listening intently. Yes, there it was again, singing, loud raucous singing, but from where at this ungodly hour of 4 am I couldn't be quite sure. I listened, fascinated, as the chorus rose and swelled, more drunken voices joining in every now and again. Some of the songs I recognised as old music-hall favourites, coming from the direction of the mess bar - apparently this was a nightly occurrence, the nearest thing to a night-club the Curragh had to offer.

The staff, Sgt. Big Jim McNamara and Cpl. Danny 'Clipper' Carlton, both single men and living in, welcomed all-comers from all over the Curragh and beyond till the late hours practically every other night. Danny was the proud possessor of a lovely tenor voice and never tired of entertaining his late night visitors, his favourite party piece being The Sergeant Major. Amazed at their nocturnal stamina, I sleepily wandered back to my own room, turned off the light and leapt into bed.

Holy Jesus! There's someone in my bed, I realised with a shock. Switching on the light, I found a body, in full uniform, curled up beneath the blankets, happily snoring his head off, a Supply & Transport lieutenant by the looks of the tabs on his shoulder, and the fumes of alcohol left no doubt where he'd been all night.

All attempts to revive him failed completely, so I just lobbed him out onto the floor, covered him with a blanket and left him there to sleep it off, not expecting to see him on his feet again for a while. Not a bit of it! Promptly at eight he arose, shook himself like a spaniel coming out of a pond, stuck out his hand and with a lop-sided grin said "Hallo! Bennett's the name. Who the fuck are you?"

I couldn't help but laugh at the sheer nerve of the man, and off he headed to wherever he was serving his country on that particular day. Apparently he'd had a fit of dropsy during the nocturnal sing-song and headed off upstairs looking for a place to throw his head and, lo and behold, there appeared my warm empty bed like a gift from heaven awaiting him.

And that's how I met Roy Bennett, one of the best friends I ever made in the army.

The colonel sat behind a polished oak desk in the middle of the room, his bald head bent over a sheaf of documents. He didn't look up as we entered, which maybe should have warned me, but I had absolutely no idea what to expect. At last he raised his eyes.

"Now listen here, young man," he growled, scowling at me under his bushy eyebrows. "I've never met you before, you're new to my command, but I've heard a lot about you" - he raised his voice a few octaves till he was almost shouting - "and everything I've heard about you has been BAAAD!"

By now he was warming to his task, his shiny scalp gleaming through the thinning strands of hair on his head. It's funny how you notice trifling unimportant things like that when your brain should more properly be paying attention to what most concerns you. He cleared his throat noisily.

"Oh, yes," he continued, "I've heard about you alright, you young pup, your reputation has preceded you. And I have only one thing to say to you." This didn't sound any too promising but I had little choice but to stand there waiting. An even longer interval followed while he allowed the full force of his words to sink in.

"You'll have to sharpen up, my lad, sharpen yourself up a whole lot. I'm giving you fair warning, this is the last time I intend to say it so you'd better pay attention. You're coming here under a cloud from Clonmel, in fact I understand they were damn glad to see the back of you." This certainly was news to me, since it was I who'd applied for a transfer out of Clonmel in the first place - but perhaps this wasn't the right time to point this out.

"So this is your last chance, young man, your very last chance to get yourself back on the right track again. If you don't straighten yourself out, buck yourself up, get a grip on yourself, I'm afraid there's only one road left for you. You're on your way out of the army!"

It's funny how all these pep-talks have the same old refrain, the same tired cliches and buzz-words which have little or no effect on those forced to listen. It's like as if they were all copied out of some thumping great manual on good behaviour written by some dull boring old clot, entitled "Confessions of a Reformed Bad Boy" or something of that nature.

To say I was a bit shocked was putting it mildly - this wasn't quite the welcome I had expected. Out of the corner of my eye I could see the pleased expressions on the faces of my new adjutant and CO, obviously delighted to see this potential new trouble-maker being put firmly in his box. But then slowly, very slowly, a surge of rage arose from the pit of my stomach at the injustice of it all. I didn't know who in Clonmel had destroyed my reputation without producing a shred of evidence, and I didn't much care either. My blood boiled. Had I anything to say - you bet I had! At least better be shot down in flames than take this kind of abuse without reply.

"Sir," I replied. "With respect, I'll see you out first".

A shocked silence fell on the room. Audible gasps came from behind me. The colonel's face turned red, then purple, his mouth opened and shut a few times before he was able to speak. "Get that man out of here," he roared. "Get him out of my sight immediately".

It was a grim-faced group that marched silently back down the road towards Connolly Barracks, with everyone now convinced that everything they'd heard about me must indeed be true - they really had trouble on their hands after all. I then had to endure a further bollocking from my own CO in his office, accompanied by dire warnings of impending doom, but at least deep down I had the satisfaction of knowing that I hadn't behaved like a sheep and let them walk all over me.

In fairness to Jim Cogan, the GOC, for all his bluster I suspect his heart wasn't really in it. I later found him to be a thoroughly decent old gent who went out of his way to make amends for our unpromising introductory meeting, no doubt having reassured himself in the meantime that I wasn't quite as bad as had been painted.

I often think more people's reputations are damned by loose talk in the bar than are ever done down by official reports, but in any case the incident never did me any harm subsequently, in fact I probably earned some grudging respect as a result.

Shortly after my arrival in the Bloods, a new CO took over. Most of Billy Kelly's career had been spent flying a desk somewhere above in GHQ or on location with film and theatre companies, but now he was being given belated command of an infantry battalion, the essential route to higher office in the army.

Short and portly, his deportment bore all the signs of the good life he'd enjoyed in all those years spent in the city. Billy was a cultured man - a patron of the arts, an expert on opera, a connoisseur of fine paintings and an epicurean of note, to which his ample girth bore witness.

He was also a keen supporter of sports and games, especially Gaelic football and the Dublin team. Hardly ever did his beloved Dubs take the field without Billy being there to cheer them on; then next day he'd treat everyone to a running commentary on the highlights of the game, boring the pants off us all. In short, Billy was a well-rounded, well-versed hedonist, who had amassed an amazingly diverse repertoire of cultural achievements throughout his life.

There was only just one problem - he knew fuckall about soldiering. He would fuss about the barracks, poking here, prying there, making enquiries about this and that and generally buzzing around like a blue-arsed fly but, alas, failing to convince the 'brutal and licentious soldiery' who have an unerring nose for such matters.

This was confirmed when the Bloods unexpectedly won all

before them in the all-army shooting competitions that year, all except one. They hacked up in the rifle, the LMG, the Gustaf, sniper and MMG, a sensational feat, but failed to win the pistol, but since the pistol was considered no big deal, nobody worried too much about the loss of one title.

Not Billy, who acted like he'd won them all himself and took the loss of the pistol personally. While these results were good, he declared, he expected the battalion to make a clean sweep the following year and training would commence as soon as the summer holidays were over. And commence it did, with special daily mental and physical exercises designed to completely sweep the boards.

Alas, when the all-army championships came around the following year our crackshots, fed up to the gills with Billy's constant badgering, failed to even raise a gallop and finished well down the field in every competition, much to his disgust. As everyone knows, you can take a horse to water......

Shortly after that, a major row broke out in the men's canteen one Friday night, which only stern action by the PAs prevented from getting out of control. Boots, belts, buckles and bottles were freely used, and when it was all over the canteen was completely wrecked and a number of men were injured, with one soldier ending up in hospital.

Bad and all as this appeared, in fact it was nothing too much out of the ordinary, just the settling of a few long-simmering disagreements which occur from time to time among fighting men cooped up together in close proximity.

At least that was the way the adjutant looked at it, since he proposed to fine the main culprit only £1 and sentence him to seven days CB (confined to barracks). Billy, however, was outraged and took over the interrogation of the man himself.

Why, he demanded to know, did the soldier start the row in the first place, injuring a comrade soldier and landing him on the flat of his back in hospital? The man hung his head, silent.

"Come now, my good man," Billy raged. "This isn't good enough, there must be a good reason why you went berserk in this fashion."

Reluctantly, the man gave his answer. He objected, he told the startled Billy, he objected strongly to something the other man had said. Delighted, Billy pressed home his advantage. This was the way to do it, he reckoned, he'd show these Curragh people how things were done up in GHQ.

"Well," he persisted. "Come on man, out with it, what was it he said?" Embarrassed, the poor fellow squirmed and turned, but Billy was relentless. Finally he cracked.

"He asked me," he stuttered, "how I was fixed for a hand-shandy."

"He what?" gasped Billy, shocked to the core. "He asked you WHAT?"

"He asked me," the embarrassed man repeated. "He asked me how I was fixed for a hand-shandy."

"Good Lord! And what did you do?" persisted Billy.

"Why, I hit him a belt, of course," the soldier replied, surprised to be asked such a stupid question. The upshot was that Billy sentenced him to do twenty one days in the glasshouse, the army prison in the Curragh, and after he'd gone, turned sadly to the adjutant.

"If there's one thing I intend stamping out in my barracks, adj," he announced. "I won't have the men drinking in the billets." And with that, out the window went soaring whatever last little bit of credibility Billy had left in the battalion.

Nine
Internment

The next few years I spent shamelessly idling away my time in the 3rd Battalion. Like it or not, you simply had to learn to live the idle life of a gentleman in order to exist, simply because there was nothing to do and all day to do it.

We'd put in the working day as best we could and then, in the evenings, we'd pass the time by playing tennis on the front lawn, head for the golf course or, much more likely, tank up in the mess bar. The majority of officers in the unit were single and living in the mess but this number was regularly swelled by some married officers posted away from home so at least there was always plenty of company.

As the only infantry unit on the Curragh, we were always on call in case of emergencies, but since nothing of any national importance was happening in the late fifties and early sixties, the battalion was let run down in strength to a shameful degree.

We endured long monotonous periods, months on end, with absolutely nothing to do - and plenty of time to get into mischief. As a result, an awful lot of heavy drinking took place, and many's the young man's career took a nose-dive through crashing boredom and stultifying inactivity.

Our predecessors on the Curragh, the British, were of course past masters in the art of idling away time with a modicum of style, having had centuries of practice in remote places like China, India, Afghanistan, Egypt and Capetown. The big difference was that their officers were normally well-heeled enough to enable them to go hunting practically every day and dine out in the poshest places at will, while our more straitened circumstances ruled that out completely. On the credit side, however, the enforced idleness of the British in these remote places spawned the invention of such weird and wonderful pastimes as cricket, soccer, croquet and polo.

We spent much of our time playing games. We had a really terrific 7-a-side football team and took part in big competitions in places like Edenderry and Straffan, where we won lots of electric razors and canteens of cutlery in a canter. Besides regular GAA stars like true Dub Mick Bohan and Corkman Barry Studdert, we also listed outstanding ball-players from other codes such as Pat McKevitt and the Douglas brothers, Seamus and Phil.

We were playing in a 7-a-side final in Edenderry, with a £200 pot for the winners, and were just ahead of the opposition and hanging on for dear life as the final minutes approached, with me lying stretched out on the ground, panting for breath and completely knackered, when Barry Studdert came thundering by and drew a kick at my prone figure as he passed.

"Get up, you lazy bastard," he roared. "There's a pair of tyres in this if we win."

Studdert had spotted my old banger of a car lying outside the mess for the past month sporting two flat back tyres and knew the right kind of pressure to apply. It was just the spur I needed. I managed to drag myself up and we went on to win the match, and within a few days, two spanking new remoulds graced my old banger and I was mobile once more.

Parties were about the only thing which relieved the boredom. Almost every month, at least one officers mess in the camp would host a social function on one pretext or another and everyone would then troop off for a fabulous night of booze and dancing and anything else you could lay your hands on.

The army always did these things very well. Young beauties from as far away as Dublin would clamour to attend although it was taboo to take them anywhere except to designated areas such as the bars and the dancefloor, still, many an illicit liaison took place out of sight in the rooms upstairs, making true the old saying 'youth will have its fling.'

At one such outing, with the very basest of motives in mind, I'd just managed to enveigle my nubile companion out into the garden for some fresh air and was preoccupied in trying to persuade her to pay an unscheduled visit to my sleeping quarters which lay on the ground floor close by the garden, when suddenly a shadowy outline hove into view.

"Here, gimme a hand," I called to the passing figure.

Obligingly, the man helped me push the somewhat reluctant lady in over the window-sill and only then did I recognise the barrack adjutant, a solid, sober, spit-and-polish type who could almost be guaranteed to greet such behaviour with a frown. A carpeting, or worse, seemed on the cards for next day, but luckily he never did a thing - maybe he'd been young himself once upon a time.

You had to look sharpish if you hoped to hold on to your girl-friend at these events, what with all the competition. I won't easily forget the day I lifted the gorgeous Pamela, the visiting skipper's young sister, at a function held in the officers mess after a rugby match. As the captain of the Curragh team, I had a headstart on all the others and fully intended to make the most of my position, and during my after-dinner speech, made full sure to include the young lady in my complimentary remarks which left her positively glowing with happiness.

The rest of the boys were green with envy, while I thought all my birthdays had come together, although I did experience some problems in beating off some very determined opposition for her attentions. At last, thinking myself secure, I dashed madly upstairs to wash and dicky myself up, lashing on generous dollops of Brut after-shave prior to taking the young lady out on the town.

Alas, when I got back down the bird had flown. The Buzzer Molloy had somehow smooth-talked her into believing that I'd been taken ill upstairs and told her I'd specifically appointed him to take care of her instead. All I could do was to grind my teeth in frustration.

To make matters worse, Buzzer insisted on waking me up in the early hours of the morning to let me know the more lurid details of his triumph. The lesson to be learnt was: where girl-friends are concerned, never trust even your best pal.

Yet despite the social restrictions which a severe lack of disposable currency induced, we still managed to live it up a storm way beyond our means. We attended every dogfight within a thirty-mile radius and when nothing else was happening, we'd throw a party ourselves. Curragh parties rightly became famous the width and breath of the country - an invitation to one of these was one to die for.

One famous night in Clarke, a gaggle of young officers from all over the army were assembled, hell-bent on action and all fired up in anticipation of a mighty 'rear-up' lasting at least half the night. Chris Dawson, the CO, a cautious man with eyes firmly fixed on the promotion list, nearly passed out when he saw the sight of the lot of us, the prospect of such uncontrollable carry-on in his mess almost causing him to have a seizure. He prudently ordered the bar closed on the dot of midnight. This almost caused a riot, but all our protests fell on deaf ears - the CO had made his decision, better safe than sorry was his motto.

A sullen silence fell on the assembled throng as the bar-shutters closed with a clang, then the waiters marched the crates of booze out between the rows of hostile young officers, under the watchful gaze of the CO, but then Christy McNamara, afterwards to die in Cyprus, made his bid for glory. Stepping smartly forward, he slapped his hand onto a passing crate and yelled out at the top of his voice, 'Bought!'

Taken by surprise, the waiters came to a halt, but then a huge cheer went up. Before you could say Jack Robinson, the cry of 'bought' was repeated in rapid succession by the other officers until the entire bar contents, crates, bottles, the lot, had been purchased. The waiters, delighted with this unexpected turn of events, promptly did an about turn and marched the crates back into the bar and the party got under way once again.

The poor CO could only look on goggle-eyed in shock at this challenge to his authority, but there wasn't a damn thing he could do about it. Finally, recognising discretion as the better part of valour, he swallowed his pride and headed off home to bed, ready to do battle another day.

The sudden introduction of internment without trial in August of 1957 was completely unexpected and caused severe disruption to the normal life of the Curragh. Internment is normally introduced only as a last resort when all other measures have failed, but in this instance it was fully justified. It was to last for five long years.

The wholesale robbing of banks on an almost daily basis, coupled with the kidnapping and holding to ransom of prominent business people in order to fund their campaign of terror and intimidation, meant that the IRA had to be stopped by whatever means possible. They had also resorted, Mafia-style, to the blatant intimidation of jury members and witnesses, even judges, which meant that normal judicial and legal procedures had to be suspended.

The old internment camp at the western end of the Curragh, previously used to house German prisoners-of-war during World War Two, was now re-opened to cater for the new political internees. Naturally enough, after all those years of disuse it was in a very poor state of repair, and a veritable army of specialist tradesmen was press-ganged into getting the place into shape as quickly as possible.

Carpenters, electricians, plumbers and painters were pulled in a swarm from all quarters and set to work with a vengeance. No expense was spared in the process, and this led to a good deal of grumbling among the troops as to why these internees, who after all were there only because they posed a threat to the state, were able to command the very best of food and clothing while we, the chosen ones, were lucky if we could get hold of an electrician to change a light-bulb socket.

But of course all this grumbling, while not exactly justified, was only to be expected. At least at the end of the day we knew we had one priceless advantage over them - we had our freedom.

Besides, if soldiers aren't cribbing and actually appear happy with their lot, then look out - something's definitely the matter!

At its peak, several hundred internees occupied the compound, and these were looked after by the military police and special personnel and so had had little or no contact with anyone on the outside. But because the internment camp had to be guarded around the clock, this put a heavy strain on the battalion's resources whose manpower was already stretched to the limit, what with bank escorts, guards for government buildings and other important installations such as power stations and communications centres. In addition to these, regular barracks and magazine duties had also to be fulfilled which led to leave being cancelled and everybody having to make themselves readily available at all times.

With all these commitments, it was obviously impossible for one battalion alone to police the internment camp properly, and so it was decided to spread the load amongst the army's other units. Even so, all of these duties, many of them of 24-hour duration, soon took a heavy toll of morale but, to their credit, the troops bore their burden manfully even if they cribbed like bloody hell.

Social life took a beating as well. Security barriers manned by armed sentries appeared as if by magic at every road junction, and identity cards had to be produced before anyone was allowed in or out.

For those living in married quarters, this presented an almost intolerable burden. Because the personnel manning the barriers changed so often, wives and children were continually stopped, questioned and searched, often on a daily basis, but they bore it all uncomplainingly.

Another casualty was the round of parties which had hitherto enlivened the otherwise grim and boring side of army life. The need to check the IDs of every incoming guest meant that numbers attending the various functions in the camp had to be severely curtailed, though this restriction failed to curtail the fun and gaiety which took place whenever circumstances allowed.

Even the military hospital, always a law unto itself as regards social functions, now had to deal with barbed wire barriers and armed sentries patrolling the grounds, making it very difficult to conduct normal hospital routine without the loss of patience or efficiency.

Nor did it just stop at barriers and security checks. Every few days, at all hours of the day and night, the general alarm would sound and all hell would break loose. First the internment camp siren would go off, followed by the siren in the magazine, then would follow the ear-splitting blast of the main siren high up in the water tower, the sound of the three sirens emitting a mournful cacophony of banshee wailing which throbbed and ebbed through every nook and cranny in the camp.

Immediately all hands would stand to. Officers, NCOs and men would pour from their messes and billets and rush headlong to the stores where the weapons and ammunition were kept under strict lock and key. As soon as everyone was armed, then would come a mad dash to take up pre-ordained positions throughout the camp while awaiting further orders.

On and inexorably on this long tedious routine extended, day after day, week after week, month after boring month without a break.

The long-anticipated break-out occurred one hot summer day in July. Everyone knew it was coming sooner or later, because all those guys had to do was sit and watch and plan, day after day after day. We could see them running round and round inside the perimeter fence and doing their daily exercises, all designed for the day when they'd make their break for freedom.

Early one misty morning, just before dawn, a group of internees managed to crawl to the perimeter fence, undetected by the sentries high above in their watch towers, cut through the barbed wire fencing and made a dash for freedom across the open plains.

Fit from constant exercising, they made ground rapidly in a bid to put themselves outside the security cordon before the alarm went off, from where they would then be spirited away by local sympathisers waiting close by.

But while the internment camp siren went off as soon as they were spotted, followed in quick succession by the one in the magazine close by, the main water-tower siren inexplicably failed to go off, thereby ensuring that several vital minutes were lost before the general alarm could be sounded.

This could only be explained by an electrical fault, whether accidental or deliberate, although an accidental breakdown was highly unlikely given the precautions which had been taken against such an eventuality.

Sure enough, the subsequent enquiry soon uncovered the culprit. A long-time employee of the Board of Works, previously considered entirely trustworthy as all such key personnel must be, was found to have betrayed the trust placed in him and to have tampered with the alarm mechanism. Fortunately for all concerned, such occurrences were rare indeed.

When finally the balloon went up, all troops in the camp stood-to under arms, while cavalry units raced outwards to establish a cordon in a bid to block off key road junctions some distance from the Curragh. Inside the cordon, search parties were organised and areas to be searched allotted, and then all the parties headed off in all directions in a co-ordinated search of likely areas.

This was slow and systematic but, though it was likely that most if not all of the escapees had flown and gone by now, there was nothing to be gained from a helter-skelter dash without careful planning. Slow but sure was the motto, and while there were some who scoffed at this modus operandi, nevertheless it paid off handsomely in the end.

My own unit, the Bloods, sent forth the largest number of search parties, one of which I commanded. I confess it came as a major shock to realise the depths of poverty which still existed in hidden pockets of rural Kildare even in the late 50s, when Ireland was considered to be reasonably prosperous.

As the long extended line of men swept through the Kildare countryside, in a broad sweep which took in everything in its path - barnyards, outhouses, garages, sheds, haystacks, dwelling-houses, even privies - I couldn't help but be stunned by the squalor to be seen. While many of the houses had washing machines and even TV, still relatively new in those days, some had only the most rudimentary furniture while others again had palettes of straw thrown down in corners acting as bedding.

Most of the people we met were friendly, supportive even, understanding the need for this type of action, but inevitably we encountered hostility and abuse here and there from dyed-in-the-wool republican supporters who loudly jeered and heckled us, calling us 'Free State lackies', 'traitors' and the like.

They took pleasure in informing us that we were wasting our time, that those we sought were beyond our reach by now, but still we soldiered on throughout that long hot day and eventually, late in the evening, our persistence paid off, when a sharp-eyed member of my team, Pte. Paddy France, spotted a bundle wrapped in camouflage sacking lying concealed in a hawthorn bush.

The figure, one of the escapees, was quickly apprehended and returned under heavily-armed escort to camp HQ, while the rest of us, now with our tails up, continued on with the search, but though we carried on long after dusk began to fall, nothing further was discovered and so we made the decision to pack up and call it a day.

It was pitch dark when we finally arrived back at barracks, from whence we had set out in the cold damp mist of early morning, to be met by the battalion adjutant standing there stiffly on the guard-room verandah. He was a recent arrival to the Bloods, having served most of his career in the relative seclusion of the Engineer Corps, and for some unknown reason went by the nickname of that famous English 17th century court diarist, the one who committed everything to paper. I was shortly to learn the reason why.

On checking in our arms and ammunition, tired and hungry but still on a high at the fairly successful conclusion of our mission, I was surprised to be told to report without delay to the adjutant's office. Pushing open the door in the fond expectation of receiving his congratulations on a difficult job well done, I instead found myself at the receiving end of a severe bollocking for not letting him know where we were going when we set out early that morning and, horror of horrors, for failing to record these details in the unit journal so that he could keep a check on our whereabouts.

The whole thing was so patently unfair and stupid that for once I was unable to conjure up a suitable reply, instead I headed for the mess bar to drown my sorrows. There to greet me was fellow-searcher Johnny Morgan, eagerly waiting to hear my story.

He greeted my tale of woe with peals of delighted laughter, before going on to explain. "Mick," said he with a broad grin. "Now you know why I christened him Samuel Pepys."

Never was a man more aptly named.

Ten
The Congo

1960 saw overseas service introduced in the Congo in the cause of the United Nations, an event which had a profound effect on the army and changed a number of things for the better. Most obvious was the substitution of smart lightweight uniforms for the old 'bulls wool' outfits which were worse than saunas in the hot tropical sun.

Ankle-high lightweight black boots replaced the old heavy-weight brown clobbers with their rows of metal studs, and a chic black beret with crimson-decked gold badge set off the army's modern new image. Lightweight tropical kit soon became standard issue for those going overseas, and the addition of a blue UN beret and neat cravat put Irish troops on an equal status with all the other nationalities.

At first things out there in the Congo were pretty cushy, with the Irish troops quickly striking up an easy-going relationship with the native Congolese, but then an incident occurred which was to have far-reaching effects.

In Niemba, on the 8th November 1961, a lightning, bloody ambush by drug-crazed Baluba tribesmen saw nine Irish soldiers killed and a number of others injured, an incident which was to traumatise the army and the nation. The story of how they were surrounded at a road block and hacked to pieces made grim reading, the only bright spot being the heartening tale of the bloodied Irish trooper staggering through the jungle for two days, arrows sticking out of his arms and back, before finally confronting a startled Irish patrol with the immortal words "Pte. Kenny reporting, sir."

The Niemba patrol was commanded by Lt. Kevin Gleeson from Kilkenny, who was in my senior cadet class and who moved heaven and earth to get himself on the Congo trip. It was just his bad luck to meet with such a horrible fate.

The Niemba ambush had another more immediate effect, however, one which was to change the laissez faire attitudes of the army forever. Gone was the easy-going rapport with the natives which had hitherto categorised the Irish, while training now took on a far more realistic edge.

The biggest change of all was in weaponry. Out went the Lee Enfield .303 mm rifle, with its long 'toasting-fork' bayonet, which had served the army well for so many years - these were now supplied to the FCA or sold overseas. Ordnance experts also travelled abroad to run the eye over possible replacement weapons designed to bring the army up to the standard required in modern warfare.

Despite hot competition from Sweden, Britain, and the US who boasted the excellent Garand model, the rifle contract was finally awarded to the Belgian company Fabrique Nationale (FN), who supplied the army with the .762mm semi-automatic rifle complete with short bayonet and the FN light machine-gun which replaced the cumbersome but reliable .303mm watercooled Vickers which had lasted almost from World War 1.

The Belgians also won the contract to supply the 9mm Browning pistol to replace the old .45 Webley revolver, while the Swedes, with their reputation for manufacturing top-grade weaponry, supplied the Gustaf sub-machine, a weapon still in service up till very recently.

The demise of the reliable old .303mm rifle was greeted with some regret. While it's true that being manually bolt-operated made it slower than a fully automatic or semi-automatic rifle, which meant each round had to be individually rammed up the breach and the expended cartridge ejected, nonetheless its solid feel made for greater accuracy at longer distances. In the final analysis, however, the greater rate of fire of the semi-automatic FN was probably the deciding factor.

Equipping the army with these weapons raised morale sky-high and gave those going overseas a new esprit-de-corps, but of course it inevitably gave an opening to some of those over-cautious administrative jackasses who afflict every organisation at moments like these.

For a few months after its issue, the short bayonet was ordered to be kept locked away in kit-boxes when not in use lest it inflict injury by its careless use, an action which didn't display much trust in such experienced men. Fortunately, these doom-sayers were quickly shouted down and put to flight and the bayonet resumed its rightful role without any serious consequences.

The Congo operation was probably the most significant event to happen in the army since the Emergency. Events overseas were followed with avid interest; regular bulletins from Army HQ supplied the most up-to-date sit-rep (situation report), while media coverage from radio, newspapers and TV kept those at home fully au fait with happenings far away.

The standard six-month period seemed to pass so quickly. No sooner had one group departed than another arrived back, filling the barracks with blue-bereted, deeply-tanned veterans laden down with presents and booty. Very soon the messes began to reflect the exotic nature of service in the Congo.

Flamboyant brightly-coloured jungle scenes painted by native artists, featuring village huts and canoes adrift on broad swirling waters, hung on walls and in hallways, while ivory elephant tusks and carved ebony heads stared balefully from every mess mantelpiece.

Since a trip overseas was about the only way to put together a nest-egg, by living on the UN allowance and banking the pay at home, competition for places was intense and people were not above using 'pull', or influence, to get themselves selected. As a result, some entirely unsuitable candidates managed to get themselves on the list despite suffering from various physical ailments; others still had problems like abuse of alcohol.

Such seemingly unimportant and trivial complaints, however, which might be tolerated here at home, assumed a far greater significance in the tropical heat under adverse conditions and with greater stress levels, and after a couple of unfortunate medical casualties, the medics became quite ruthless in weeding out those who weren't category A.1.

The dental hut in those early days resembled nothing less than scenes from an abattoir. The few army dentists available were quite unable to cope with the sheer workload in the short time to hand. Squads of men were marched in at one end of the dental hut every day, every bad or even half-dodgy tooth was yanked unceremoniously out, and the bloodied victims were briskly marched out the other end again.

It was real assembly-line stuff. No question of fillings or saving any teeth for posterity, no appreciation of keeping up cosmetic appearances - if you wanted to travel overseas, out those game teeth had to come. Reserve dentists were called up to handle the overflow, my old boyhood friend and fellow-cadet Michael McCarthy from Abbeyside among them, though the situation did improve as the service expanded.

But even among those lucky ones selected to travel, casualties were not unknown. Quite a few went on such a celebratory 'bender' that they had to be de-selected for their own good, others again encountered family problems, while chaplains sometimes exerted pressure where an overseas trip threatened to break up a man's marriage.

In the Congo, the Niemba ambush was followed soon afterwards by the battle for Jadotville, an event which left a long-term bad flavour in the army. Jadotville is a small town about the size of Mullingar, situated about seventy miles from Elizabethville, the capital of mineral-rich Katanga province.

In July 1961, C Company of the Irish battalion, under the command of Commdt. Pat Quinlan, was surrounded and attacked by thousands of Katangese gendarmerie commanded by Belgian officers and bolstered by the addition of several hundred foreign mercenaries.

For five days and nights the battle raged; here at home everyone went around with transistor radios glued to their ears, the progress of the battle the sole topic of conversation, and when it was all over, the Irish had surrendered and had been imprisoned and were being guarded by heavily armed gendarmes.

Even worse, a platoon from the Bloods also surrendered, and when a photograph appeared on the front pages of some newspapers showing several of our soldiers surrounded by armed blacks, laughing and waving flags and looking for all the world as if they'd just won the cup, the mood in the battalion was sombre.

The slogans on the flags clearly read "Up the Bloods", and it was painfully obvious that our men were unarmed while their Congolese captors, grins of triumph lighting up their sweaty black faces, brandished their weapons menacingly. After a shocked silence, everyone retired to the bar in disgust for the rest of the day to drown our sorrows - it was indeed a black day for the battalion.

While we didn't know the full details of the surrender, I well remember my feelings of shame, rage even, at the Jadotville garrison's craven unwillingness to fight on. I simply couldn't imagine myself surrendering, chucking in the towel like that, no matter what the situation, and I wasn't alone in my views.

Surrender is always a dirty word among soldiers, but when it involved the first recorded surrender of white troops to ill-trained blacks, the shame was almost too much to bear.

However, outright condemnation was tempered by the realisation that no-one can accurately predict how he will behave when he himself is faced with his moment of truth, which is inclined to modify any gung-ho attitudes.

Eventually the survivors returned home, to be greeted by a torchlight procession through the streets of Athlone. The rest of us couldn't seem to appreciate how these townspeople could even dream of celebrating such a humiliation, instead of allowing the survivors to slink quietly home and keep a low profile, but perhaps they knew something we didn't.

Gradually memories of the affair slowly died away, to be hidden in the merciful mists of time, only surfacing when jeers and taunts caused the occasional flare-up in bars and canteens throughout the army. Most people were happy to let the matter lie, though feelings of contempt still lay pretty close beneath the civilised surface. Thereafter Jadotville remained a closed subject.

Eleven
The Sergeant Major

But even while the Congo operation was going on, little or no fresh blood was being recruited into the army. Life became an endless grind of duties, duties and more duties, mainly barrack and magazine guard, with the odd internment camp stint thrown in for good measure. This placed a heavy burden on the NCOs and men and morale suffered badly as a result. Since most of these duties entailed twenty-four hours at a stretch and occurred sometimes as often as twice a week, sporting and social activities were badly hit, not to mention the men's married lives.

My own company comprised just one man, even though we had a full complement of officers and NCOs, and it looked absolutely ridiculous when we marched out on parade, with the company commander standing out in front, three subalterns just behind, the two company NCOs next, and a lone solitary soldier bringing up the rear.

Needless to say, the politicians didn't really give a fiddlers, as long as they got security on the cheap they weren't really worried. But in spite of everything the unit still managed to train machine-gunners, mortarmen, anti-tank gunners and riflemen up to their usual high standard, and even managed to pull off the occasional win in the all-army shooting championships which were held on the Curragh ranges every summer.

This was in no small measure due to the NCOs of the battalion. Officers came and went, but the NCO core remained more or less intact, and to these loyal, hard-drinking men most of the credit for holding the line is due.

No matter what job they took on or what sport they competed in, whether football, hurling, boxing, shooting or gymnastics, the whole battalion turned out to cheer on their heroes. Men like The Red Connolly, Red Doyle and Punchy Dowling came to epitomise what the Bloods stood for - courage and a refusal to admit defeat.

'Hooker' Regan more than any other man summed up the Bloods' never-say-die attitude. Hooker was probably the best-known private in the entire army due to the rugby prowess gained in his youth in his native Limerick, but he was also an outstanding soccer player and, with Wally Barnes, one of the reasons why we had one of the defence forces' best soccer teams. It was privates like these, in addition to first-class NCOs, who made the 3rd one of the best units in the entire army and enabled it to survive often indifferent leadership over the years.

It can truthfully be said that the rank of sergeant major is probably the most important rank in any unit. He's the main link between the commissioned officers and the NCOs and men, and is the CO's trusted confidant in keeping the wheels running smoothly.

Everyone has his own image of what a 'sarn major' should be like. Big and brash, with a bristling moustache, he should lift the hair on your head when he roars and turn the air blue while putting the fear of God into everyone around him.

The old music-hall song says it best:
"Pick 'em up, pick 'em up there,
That's the way I'm made,
Pick 'em up, pick 'em up there,
If you don't you'll hear me call a spade a spade.

NCOs say I bite,
While recruits die of fright,
When the Sergeant Major's on parade."

Our sergeant major was cut from a different cloth altogether. While the majority of the others tried to live up to their image as tough, no-nonsense tyrants, Danny Douglas presented a far more civilised face to the world. Not for him the bawling and bellowing that characterised the likes of 'The Liver' Dunne - he was far too intelligent for that. In these more enlightened days Danny almost certainly would have been selected for a commission, but back then he settled for doing an important job with the minimum of fuss.

He never ever came the heavy on anyone under him, he didn't have to; but if perchance someone didn't fancy the idea of responding to his quiet, respectful suggestions, he had his own ways of enforcing his authority. As a result he was not only extremely popular, but highly respected as well.

The CO, Charley Doherty, was himself very partial to a few drinks, and the officers mess bar hardly ever closed while there was anyone there to keep it open, which was often till parade time the following morning. But the motto was, if you can't take it, don't drink it - by hook or by crook, drunk or sober, you had to be on parade next morning and get on with the job with the minimum of messing.

Every morning about ten, Charley was in the habit of heading over to the NCOs mess for a cure, since they served the best pint of Guinness in the whole camp. Normally there wouldn't be anyone there but the mess sergeant and himself, so he'd be able to enjoy his drink and read the papers to his heart's content before heading off on his tour of the barracks in the company of the sergeant major.

This particular morning, after an especially hard session the night before, he was really looking forward to his morning cure in peace, and was a bit taken aback to find the sergeant major and a few senior NCOs there before him, sipping gingerly on their pints. They had had a big tally-ho the previous night as well and were in a very fragile state indeed when Charley unexpectedly walked in.

The other NCOs didn't know where to look or what to do with embarrassment but Douglas, urbane as ever, quickly came to the rescue.

"Good morning, sir," he chirruped smoothly. "And what'll you have?"

But Charley wasn't having any of this kind of palaver. "I'll tell you what I'll have, sarn major," he growled. "I'll have your number, rank and name, that's what I'll have!"

Now this was the normal method of telling you that you were about to put on a disciplinary charge sheet and was very bad news indeed. Quick as a flash, Danny gathered his wits about him.

"Right-o men," he announced briskly. "That's the end of this conference. Dismiss!" And leaving their half-finished pints on the table, they all marched briskly out, saluting the CO as they went. All he could do was gape after them.

"You know," he confided with a chuckle to the adjutant during coffee break later on. "That Danny Douglas is a smart operator and no mistake!" Which was about as high a compliment as he could ever pay him.

Shortly afterwards, I was packed off to undergo a PT course in the Army School of Physical Culture, which meant I would be away from all regular barrack duties for a period of at least six months. The only other one to be sent from our unit was Sgt. Dan O'Driscoll, and we both entered into the swing of things with great enthusiasm.

Big Dan was a genial giant of a man, with a pair of huge blue eyes set in a deeply-tanned face, topped off by a shock of jet-black hair and a broad west-Cork accent you could cut with a knife. He also had a very short fuse, and the men liked nothing better than to tease him.

They had a nickname for him, 'The Beast', which they delighted in broadening so that it came out sounding something like 'Baaayssht'! Needless to say, nobody ever called him that to his face, but the men would tease him unmercifully and would yell out 'Baaayssht' from the safety of the balconies as he passed nearby.

Dan never failed to rise to the bait, and with a roar of rage would charge wildly up the stairs cursing and swearing and issuing dire threats, but by then his tormentors would have long since disappeared in every direction - wouldn't you?

Class-taking was the single most important part of the PT course, and for the final tests squads of noisy kids were sent down from the local school to provide authentic material. Dan of course had been severely warned to curb his quick temper, and was on his very best behaviour as he faced up to take his class, right in front of the testing board which sat at tables close by the wall.

But by this time the young boys were getting restless and fed up with all this carry-on and, like youngsters all over, were inclined to play a few pranks. Gritting his teeth, Dan over-looked the first few bits of deliberate messing, but when one clumsy lad tripped another during a forward roll and caused him to make a complete hames of the exercise, and the class exploded with laughter, he lost the head completely.

"Oi you, you snotty-nosed little bugger," he bellowed, red-faced with rage. "Get out here immediately and do three press-ups, just for acting the c..t!" The shocked looks on the faces of the testing board said it all, and soon after Big Dan was on his way back to his unit, to try again another day.

Soon afterwards, a small group of us set up a Freedom From Hunger committee in the Curragh, the very first of its kind in Ireland and the forerunner to such as Gorta and Concern. It was great fun and attracted people like Roger McCorley and Gerry Gosling, who demonstrated their great flair and organisational skills to good effect. Over a period of a few years we organised a series of highly-successful functions, including the Derby Ball, which is still happily in existence.

A number of civilians were also roped in to lend their exper-tise - people like Una McCann, whose husband Dick died in the Congo, and Sean Cleary, PRO of Irish Ropes, whose mar-keting skills were invaluable in getting our message across.

Sadly, all this laudable effort had to be discontinued when Jimmy Quinn, the GOC, forbade any further help from any army source and, since we depended greatly on the army's help with things like locations, manpower and transport, carrying on seemed pointless. The committee disbanded shortly afterwards.

The reason he gave was that our efforts should first and foremost be devoted to raising funds for the Army Benevolent Fund, which I suppose was a fair enough point. He objected most strongly, the GOC maintained, to money leaving the country which should more properly be spent relieving poverty here at home.

Charity begins at home, was his motto, and rightly so - but of course the answer to that is that it doesn't end there. I found it extraordinary that a man as decent and honourable as the GOC undoubtedly was should have developed so limited an overall view, but I suppose we all have our blind spots.

In all the years since it was first put up for competition, nobody had ever managed to beat the General Training Depot in the annual athletics contest in the Curragh, but now we laid out a plan to relieve them of the magnificent solid silver shield and remove it to Connolly Barracks for the first time in history.

The GTD had always had the assistance of the semi-professional gym staff and were considered unbeatable, so everyone in our battalion who could make any kind of a shape at all was pressed into service in the hope of winning a precious point.

First of all Sgt. Dan Driscoll hacked up in the weights events, the 56 lbs without follow and the 56 over the bar, followed by his sidekick Sgt. Christy Reidy who managed to scrape second place, thus securing some very valuable points, then Dan garnered points in the hammer, shot and discus, and we were on our way.

A couple of privates picked up another few precious points in the sprints and jumps before John Mackey, our cross-country star, made hacks of the field in the distance events. All it needed now was for me to come up trumps in the jumps and field events and, to the delight of the whole battalion, the trophy was on its way to the Bloods.

We had it won before they fully realised it, and it gave me one of the greatest thrills in my whole career to hang the shield on the wall in Connolly mess, leaving a great dirty brown stain on McDonagh Officers Mess ante-room wall where it had hung all those years, which compelled them to wallpaper the entire room shortly afterwards.

That was a great day.

Twelve
His Master's Voice

An aide-de-camp (ADC) is usually the commanding officer's right-hand man, responsible, among other things, for ensuring he keeps his appointments and shielding him from unwelcome attention, but oftentimes, as a result of his position, people would credit him with wielding far greater influence with his boss than he actually does, and of course this wouldn't prevent him from 'taking the mickey' out of his pals from time to time.

Mick Harrington was a prime example. A born trickster, he'd regularly ring up a friend, announce himself importantly as some VIP or other and then, before the misfortunate chap had managed to cop on, proceed to give him an unmerciful bollocking over the phone. But like most pranksters, Mick cried 'wolf' once too often, and pretty soon the word got around and he began receiving hoax calls himself, and since he simply hated being made the victim of such hoaxes, this naturally made him suspicious of every telephone call he received.

One morning early, while all the officers were busy at breakfast in Ceannt mess, the phone rang and rang, but the mess staff were too busy serving and it went unattended for some time. Eventually, after an age, it was picked up by a passer-by, and the conversation went something like this:

Chief of Staff (for it was he) - "Hallo. This is the Chief of Staff."

Voice (in a rich Kerry accent) - "Yeah, and this is Ho Chi Minh."

Chief - "I beg your pardon?"

Voice - "I said this is Ho Chi-fucking Minh."

A pause.

Chief - "Who's speaking, please?"

Voice - "Ha ha ha, you won't catch me out like that."

A longer pause. Then the COS's voice again, this time heavy with menace.

Chief - "THIS... IS... THE... CHIEF... OF... STAFF... SPEAKING. Who is this, please?"

An even longer pause at the Ceannt end while the awful truth slowly dawned. Silence.

Chief (outraged) - "Do you know who this is?"

Voice - "No."

Chief - "This is the Chief of Staff!"

Voice - "Do you know who this is?"

Chief - "No."

Voice - "Well good luck so!"

And placing the receiver gently back into its slot, the man with the Kerry voice made himself scarce in a hurry, leaving the Chief of Staff foaming at the mouth on the other end. Of course Harrington always swore it wasn't him, but in the words made famous by Mandy Rice-Davies - "Well, he would, wouldn't he!"

Commanding officers annual inspections in those days were always a bit of a carnival. Days and weeks beforehand would be spent in preparation; scuffing and weeding, polishing and painting, cleaning and shining, till the entire barracks looked spick and span.

The Colonel would always take the parade on the main square, to the sound of raucous bellowing and martial music, personally inspecting every available man while his staff went through the administration records with a finecomb. The inspection over, the troops would march past the saluting dais where the Colonel took the salute, then off the entire inspection entourage would go off to inspect billets, weapon stores, cookhouse, ration stores and finally the QM's clothing stores.

Every single room would be looked at, nothing was allowed to be locked away or concealed. For days beforehand all spare junk and buckshee equipment would be spirited away and hidden in some secure place in case the GOC asked some awkward questions.

The inspection itself was a howl to watch. The caravan would descend on a small, cramped, dingy little store hidden away somewhere at the back of the barracks and then, while the sole occupant stood stiffly to attention, everyone would try to crowd in after the GOC, causing a major traffic jam in the process.

First would come the orderly officer and escort leading the way, then the GOC and aide-de-camp, accompanied by the barracks OC and second in command, followed by the camp adjutant and camp quartermaster. Next would come the barracks adj and QM and their assistants, then the company commander and company sergeant, with the CQMS bringing up the rear.

The whole winding elongated worm would then attempt to push its way into the tiny stores, with those behind struggling hardest to cram in, in case the GOC asked them a question, and in the process jamming those inside who were trying to get back out. It would have been laughable if it wasn't so pathetic.

And if perchance the colonel asked a man a question, complete panic would set in. Before he'd have a chance to answer, half a dozen people behind would try to get in on the act. Any criticism would be expertly fielded by the barracks OC, who'd deftly turn it over to the adj, who'd then pass it on to the QM, who in turn would leave it to his CQMS, who'd finally mutter something like "the CO knows about that, sir," and scribble something unintelligible in his notebook.

The GOC, not expecting an answer in any case, would nod and go stomping out the door, in the process tripping over the people outside who were still struggling to get in, like something you'd see in a Laurel and Hardy film.

In the meantime, the unit quartermaster sergeants would be hovering anxiously at the back, straining their ears to try to anticipate the GOC's latest whim. One CQMS, Wally Keegan, a wily old fox, on learning that DDT was the current rave, sent a messenger racing post-haste on his bicycle to the cookhouse for flour, fistfuls of which were then liberally sprinkled all over the store blankets.

He then had the cheek to stand there smirking smugly while the GOC warmly complimented him on his perspicacity in being the only CQMS in the whole camp to use DDT in his stores.

Finally, to end the day, a conference to thrash out problems, followed by a big feed of grub and a few drinks, then the whole caboodle would pack up and go home, ready to hit another unit another day.

Colonel Tony Lawlor was a throwback to the pukkha-sahib days of the old Indian Raj and one of the more colourful GOCs ever to govern the Curragh. He arrived to join up in the early days of Ireland's fledgling army via the Royal Flying Corps where he served for a number of years, and he never really lost the British love-affair with parades and colourful pageants.

A bristling Jimmy Edwardes-type moustache covered the lower half of his florid face, a monocle being about the only thing missing in order to complete the Colonel Blimp image.

To placate him on parade, all you had to do was to bellow out orders in as loud a voice as possible while the troops tried to dig a hole in the square with their boots.

But aside from all that vim and polish, Tony was a very sociable man who strongly believed in promoting a lively mess life in the camp, together with his wife, who was affectionately known as 'Mrs. Camp'. He was also a hands-on type who believed in leading by example. He'd hit a different mess every night and stay there till the wee small hours, waffling away on first-name terms to the lowest second lieutenant as if they had known one another all their lives.

Next morning, however, was a different kettle of fish - 'on duty, on duty; off duty, off duty' was his motto, and woe betide anyone who dared display any familiarity whatsoever next day. Besides, most mornings he'd be like a bear with a sore arse due to a hangover, so it would be at least midday before anyone even dared approach him.

One St. Patrick's Day morning, Tony was driving past the Depot on his way to work in camp HQ, when out of the corner of his eye he spotted the 'Cocker' Daly, the Depot OC, distributing shamrock to the troops lined up on the square.

Now the Cocker was a meek, gentle, religious man who wouldn't say 'boo' to a goose, and whatever it was that attracted Tony's attention no-one will ever know, but with a loud screech of brakes, the car lurched to a halt right in front of the troops, and out Tony hopped, spitting fire and fury, and straight away laid into the astounded Cocker.

"What the devil d'you think you're doing, man?" Tony roared, face flushed with rage. "That's not the proper way to distribute shamrock."

Before the Cocker had a chance to reply, Tony suddenly lashed out with his crop and sent the box of shamrock flying up into the air, whereupon the wind quickly blew it tumbling away down the square in the direction of the military college, vainly chased by a bevvy of eager staff types. Then, uttering fiery snorts of rage, he quickly turned on his heel and stomped away towards his car, bellowing as he went "This is a bloody circus!"

For a moment everyone stood transfixed, stunned by the sheer suddenness of the affair, but then, to everybody's complete amazement, the Cocker took off across the square, catching up with Tony just before he could get into his car.

"This may be a circus, all right," he shouted, in his sharp Northern accent. "But if it is, then you're the chief bloody clown!"

A gasp of surprise went up at this unexpected display of spunk, since the Cocker had never been known to raise his voice to anyone before in his life. Tony too got a shock, standing there open-mouthed for a few seconds, before roaring off in his car, wheels spinning wildly.

But Tony was nothing if not a big man, and his opinion of the Cocker was probably higher than ever when he'd managed to cool down. It wasn't too very long before he appeared in person to apologise. For all his fiery temper, he was a thorough gentleman at heart and was never known to do anyone a bad turn in his entire career which, if you think about it, is not such a bad epitaph for any man.

Christmas was Tony's favourite time. He'd make a habit of trying to visit every canteen and mess in the camp on Christmas morning just to wish the troops the compliments of the season in person, but since every barracks had at least two messes and one canteen, this added up to an awful lot of visits. Worse still, it was customary for each mess to offer the GOC a generous seasonal 'ball of malt' before he departed, which, being a gentleman, Tony would never dream of refusing.

He'd start at one end of the camp and slowly try to work his way down to the other, but by the time he reached the half-way point at the water-tower he'd be under severe pressure, even though there was never any question of him quitting. Then suddenly, halfway through a speech, his legs would slowly buckle beneath him and he'd slide gently to the floor, out for the count, but since this was only to be expected, no one ever took any offense, and he'd then be gently carted off home by willing hands, 'Mrs Camp' in close attendance, to enjoy his Christmas dinner in his own warm bed.

They don't make 'em like that anymore.

Thirteen
Eileen Works a Miracle

Sometime in the early sixties, Sean Berry and myself resurrected the rugby club in the Curragh, which for some strange reason had fallen away badly in the years after the war. The club competed mostly in the Provincial Towns Cup, playing against the surrounding towns in Leinster.

We had a policy of playing unusual opponents wherever they could be found. One of the most extraordinary of these was The Honourable Artillery Company, a London-based club with whom we became quite friendly. The HAC have a charter from Charles 1, and own their own ground right in the heart of the City which must now be worth a fortune on the property market.

The HAC were a most amazing bunch. Many were men of substance in London, lawyers, stock-brokers, politicians and the like, but when on duty with the Honourable Company, which loosely resembles something like our own FCA, their identities were subsumed into the usual menial tasks of an army outfit. Their cook sergeant, for example, was a prominent barrister who regularly held forth at Old Bailey murder trials.

Unable to find anyone else in Ireland to give them a game and justify a weekend spree in Ireland, they got in touch with the Curragh who took them on with some trepidation, but it was such a success that very quickly the fixture became an annual affair on a home and away basis.

Despite their elevated social status back home, they were a joy to look after. We put them up in rough and ready billets whenever mess accommodation was limited but they never raised a murmur, in fact they seemed to enjoy it all.

I still recall the stunned looks in the crowd at half-time as a couple of flunkeys in top hat and tails marched briskly on to the pitch carrying trays of glasses and buckets containing bottles of iced champagne - the only way to live! Regrettably the HAC fixture had to be discontinued due to the deteriorating security situation, but hopefully it will be revived just as soon as circumstances permit.

The majority of our other engagements were mundane except for the Towns Cup, though there were also exhibition matches, and it was in one of these that I got my first lesson on international forward power. The Curragh Selected XV, with myself as captain, was playing against the President's XV, which included a fair sprinkling of international players and celebrities, among them famous prop Ray McLoughlin and Tony O'Reilly.

The match was proceeding in an orderly and dignified fashion, with nothing serious at all happening and myself modelling nicely at full back and keeping out of trouble as best I could, when out of the blue a scrum developed about twenty yards from our line.

Suddenly a phalanx of huge beefy forwards disengaged and surged towards our endline, obviously intent on scoring the try which would break the scoring deadlock and win themselves the handsome trophies which went to the winners. With sinking heart I focussed on the front three charging towards me, Ray McLoughlin in the middle, flanked on either side by PJ Dwyer and Locky Butler, all of them either internationals or interpros.

"Holy Jesus," I thought to myself. "I'm going to get stuffed!"

I'm told your whole life flashes before your eyes in that last vital moment before destruction - mine certainly did. With thoughts of avoiding nemesis uppermost, I wondered guiltily if anyone would notice if I put in a dummy tackle? After all, this was only an exhibition and I was expected to make a speech at the dinner afterwards - but deep down I knew they would notice and I'd never be let forget it for the rest of my life.

Bravely I put such treasonous thoughts out of my mind and comported myself to confront the three great brutes now bearing down hard upon me. I was greatly relieved to see that McLoughlin, the most fearsome of the three, had now passed the ball to Dwyer and, gritting my teeth, I crash-tackled him as hard as I could.

That was the last I remember. I awoke fifteen minutes later lying on the sideline surrounded by the medics, blood pouring from my nose and a million stars spinning in front of my eyes.

I learned later that the heartless brute, on seeing me coming, had simply dipped his shoulder and bulldozed his way over the line for a try, taking me with him as if I didn't exist. It was a major effort to speak at the dinner later on, my jaw ached so much, and for years afterwards my rib-cage hurt every time I laughed or took a deep breath, but I consoled myself with the thought that, bad though Dwyer was, it could have been even worse - I might have tackled McLoughlin!

The Towns Cup matches, while not as tough as playing against the big boys, were still pretty rough and the occasional serious injury could still occur. Going down on the ball during a forward rush against Wicklow Town in the cup, our fullback, Dougie McManus, received a kick on the base of the spine which left him lying prostrate on the ground when the ruck broke up. Shrewdly suspecting the injury might be serious, the referee suspended the game until an ambulance arrived and Dougie was carted off to hospital.

It transpired that the injury was indeed serious - he had a fractured spine which left him completely paralysed below the waist. Our own army doctors were really worried about his injury, and plans were made to transfer him to the National Rehabilitation Centre in Dun Laoire if his condition didn't quickly improve.

The biggest problem was that Dougie's bowels just wouldn't work, so the doctors had to resort to every trick in the book to try to stimulate him to perform. Twice every day for a week, a great big wooden privy was wheeled into the ward, he'd be lifted on, and water noisily poured from jug to jug to try to jog his memory. Nothing succeeded.

All this would have been really funny if it wasn't so serious, though of course this didn't prevent his pals from cruelly teasing him, humourously suggesting that it was a waste of time trying to stimulate his senses anyway since everyone knew he'd been brain dead for years!

The final day of trying arrived. If nothing worked that day, there would remain no option but to cart him off to rehab in Dun Laoire to see if anything could be done for him there. Chris Haverty and Nancy Corrigan, his two nurses, valiantly laboured away doing their level best, pouring water, pressing his tummy, and simulating various sound effects, but all to no effect. The mood in the ward was gloomy.

Then in marched Sister Eileen Graham, the resident religious guru, festooned with a plethora of crucifixes and rosary beads plus a few miraculous medals as well. The doctors stared in surprise, wondering what she had to say that might be of help.

"I was wondering," Eileen began timidly, "I was wondering if you'd let me rub Dougie's leg with a relic of Blessed Martin?"

Everyone gazed blankly, but no-one dared laugh outright. After all, when all was said and done, Eileen was a good and saintly person who believed implicitly in the power of prayer. She also had a particular devotion to Blessed Martin de Tours, patron saint of hopeless cases - and if this wasn't a hopeless case, what was?

Reluctantly, Dougie gave his permission, and why not? After all, everything else had been tried, and a drowning man will clutch at straws. The mood was sombre as the nurses pulled down the legs of his pyjamas and Eileen approached. With great reverence, she touched his unfeeling buttocks with the saintly relic, blessing herself the while, then gently withdrew. The others, meanwhile, struggled manfully to suppress their mirth lest they give offence.

But as soon as she was gone, all restraint disappeared. The

room exploded with laughter as the tension dissolved. Doctors, nurses, medical orderlies, everyone laughed and laughed till they cried, rocking up and down, holding their sides as howls of mirth filled the room.

And poor Dougie laughed most of all, in spite of his discomfort, tears running down his cheeks at the memory of Sister Eileen and her pathetic faith in divine providence.

But then, lo and behold, if a miracle didn't occur! With a loud burst of flatulence, Dougie's hitherto dormant disposal organs suddenly burst into life, leaving him wrapped in painful contortions in the middle of the bed. The others could only gape in astonishment.

The good tidings spread like wildfire from the hospital throughout the Curragh, and crowds of his friends lined up to offer their congratulations. Flowers and chocolates piled up beside his locker, and the wooden privy was quietly banished to the backroom closet, never to be taken out for Dougie again.

As for Eileen, well, she took it all calmly and smiled and thanked God, and Blessed Martin, for Dougie's cure. You can say what you like, and the sceptics did, and blame it on hypnotism, auto-suggestion or whatever, but whichever way you care to look at it, who's to say it really wasn't a miracle?

Ask Dougie!

The thing I found hardest to stomach was the clique of senior staff officers which assembled every time anyone anywhere got into a spot of bother. They'd come running from all directions, the same gang every time, to pick over the bones of the poor fellow who was in trouble - but with no question of anyone of them offering to help. I found it difficult to respect that particular bunch of toadies.

Part of the problem was that the CO and myself were simply incompatible - it happens, and there's little that can be done about it. Nicknamed Con John, and a cavalryman, he had this pathetic fixation with spit and polish, short

Prussian-style haircuts, slashed peaked caps and all that kind of jazz, which is all very well and of course has its place but which can be overdone and brought to the other extreme.

Like many people not quite up the job, he and his cohorts were sticklers for spit and polish and petty quotidian things. In lieu of a biting intellect, he had accumulated an armoury of key-words, such as 'discipline', 'responsibility' and 'duty', which he spat out like machine-gun bullets to impress; but if perchance you still refused to be cowed by the totem words, he'd completely lose the head and try the iron fist instead.

I well remember his apoplectic fit of rage when, having reprimanded me for what he perceived to be a hairstyle too long, I pointed out that the Germans, who always had close-cropped heads, lost the last two World Wars, whereas the British, whose officers sported notably flowing locks, won them. Not surprisingly, these views of mine weren't exactly appreciated.

Besides, all this business of tight haircuts belongs completely in the past. Short haircuts were only made mandatory during the Crimean War and other such campaigns when disease and head-lice were rampant, but these days better hygiene has largely eliminated that risk. You'd have to be kinda suspicious of people who continually harp on about tight haircuts and stuff like that to the exclusion of other more important matters.

I recall with particular distaste the reign of terror which obtained in the Cadet School in the early sixties, when a new Cadet Master instituted a regime of US-style crew-cuts which would have shamed Sing Sing prison. Not content with just hounding the unfortunate cadets, over-zealous NCOs even attempted to spread the campaign to the hapless privates of the college company but they, to their credit, resisted fiercely. Perhaps inevitably, as a result of all the pressure, absenteeism and desertion among the men became rife.

So it came as no great surprise when I was asked to defend a Pte. Houlihan from the college company on a court martial charge of refusing to obey a lawful order. It was normal enough practice for an officer to act as defence counsel when the charges were not too serious or if the accused didn't feel like hiring a lawyer.

The crime Houlihan was accused of was refusing to get a No.1, or a 'regulation' haircut, when ordered to do so by the sergeant major. I don't quite know why he chose me to defend him - perhaps because my own locks were conspicuously long - but more likely it was because I'd sparred with him in the boxing ring a couple of times during his days as a recruit in the depot.

Houlihan, from Dundalk, came from the rough side of the tracks, but I found him to be an excellent lad if handled properly. Fellows like him often are used only to being shouted at and abused, but I've found that they usually respond to being treated fairly. Houlihan was especially proud of his shock of wavy brown hair which he kept in immaculate condition at all times.

In any event, I quickly set out to mount as robust a defence as I possibly could, feeling strongly as I did that the men of the college company were being unfairly 'ridden'. A prosecution witness, a college sergeant, gave evidence to the court that he'd ordered Houlihan to get a haircut, but later on spotted him attempting to slip out of barracks without having done so. He again ordered him to get a 'regulation' haircut but he refused, saying that he'd already got a haircut, that he was only just out of hospital and was going home to Dundalk on three weeks sick leave. Instead of going on sick leave, however, poor Houlihan found himself slapped into the guardroom for his pains, charged with the offense of refusing to obey a lawful order.

The first man I called for the defence was the college barber, who testified that he had in fact given Houlihan a haircut as requested. He also testified that, in his opinion, the haircut given was perfectly in line with the norm. He hadn't given a No.1 or 'regulation', he said, because Houlihan had told him he was going on sick leave and didn't want to have it too tight.

Next into the box was the main witness, the sergeant major

himself, who testified that he had twice ordered Houlihan to get a No. 1 haircut, an order which he'd refused, leaving him no option but to incarcerate him in the guardroom in the interests of maintaining discipline.

It soon became obvious that, because he'd been a desk wallah all his life, the sergeant major was completely out of his depth in this job and was just a hand-picked clone who'd do anything to ingratiate himself further with the Cadet Master. It was also obvious he hadn't done his homework - now it was time to go for the jugular.

Asked if he was familiar with the term a 'No. 1 haircut', he replied that of course he was, as indeed he was with any part of army regulations. A No. 1 or 'regulation' haircut meant a short back and sides, with an inch of hair or less on top. Pressed as to which regulation this actually was, he replied that he couldn't say for sure but it was certainly one he was very familiar with, one he'd seen many times during the course of his army career, but then, with a triumphant flourish, I presented him with a copy of the DFRs (defence force regulations) and invited him to demonstrate to the court which regulation and where.

For what seemed an age, he hummed and hawed, squirmed and twisted, evaded and prevaricated, flicking through the pages as if mesmerised, but all to no avail. It was pitiful to watch and in the end I even felt a little sorry for him, but the plain fact was that no such regulation existed in the DFRs. While the term had probably crept into common usage over the years, in reality there was no such thing as a No. 1 or a 'regulation' haircut.

And now it was time to nail the opposition to the cross. A succession of privates from the college company came forward to testify that they fiercely resented being forced to get a No. 1 haircut because they were jeered and laughed at and their girlfriends refused to go out in public with them. Worse still, NCOs constantly harried them to get a No. 1, sometimes even during mealtimes. The court didn't seem very impressed with this kind of carry-on.

The upshot of it all was that the charges against Houlihan

were dismissed in full, and the court added a rider severely reprimanding the college authorities for unjust harassment of the men. Furthermore, it recommended that the practice of giving No.1 or 'regulation' haircuts should be immediately discontinued throughout the entire Military College, leaving the Cadet Master and his sergeant major with egg on their faces. It was a famous victory, one which gave me great personal satisfaction and which was celebrated with gusto in the men's canteen in the Military College.

But alas, it was all in vain. Before a full month was out, poor Houlihan was again in trouble, unmercifully harassed and harried for one thing or another until he finally cracked and deserted. And after that the unfortunate barber, who had given evidence on his behalf, was also targeted and got well and truly hammered.

Before long, I also had to defend him on trumped-up court martial charges, which were dismissed, but eventually he too went on his 'ticket', unable to take it any more. The whole affair truly was a scandal, but there was nothing I nor anyone else could do to stop it.

Only once did I ever see Houlihan again, in the Simon Community some years later while taking part in some voluntary work. He was by then in a pretty shabby state and suffering badly from the effects of too much alcohol, but he still greeted me warmly and we had a great laugh reminiscing over the court martial and how we did the bastards down. We promised to keep in touch, but sadly I never saw him again.

I often think of that poor fellow and in hindsight wish I had done more, but without the security of a good job and a steady hand to guide him, perhaps it was inevitable that a fellow like Houlihan, from a rough area and with little education, and carrying a big chip on his shoulder, would end up as a driftwood statistic in some lonely doss-house somewhere. It was just his luck to run up against the kind of cruel regime and twisted people, little Hitlers who abused their powers, that people only read about in novels.

Ever since then I have misgivings about people with tight-cropped hair, while there are even some people who persist in equating long hair with some forms of depravity.

Some years ago one of these martinet-types was dispatched as administrative officer to the Air Corps, having spent a number of years in the GTD. On his arrival in Baldonnel, he almost had a seizure when he saw the state of their men whom he considered total muck-birds, and promptly set to work to change that situation as fast as he could, and pretty soon the list of privates on charge sheets for haircuts and scruffy turnouts was as long as a wet week. Absenteeism and desertions, hitherto almost unknown, now began to rise rapidly.

It was obvious this situation couldn't be allowed to continue. If he continued to harass the men like that, who could answer for the consequences, especially with regard to flying safety. Soon someone had a quiet word with the Air Corps supremo about all the unnecessary harassment, and shortly afterwards our martinet was on his way back to the Curragh and his beloved GT Depot.

The question was: which was the more important - spit-and-polish, or aeronautical efficiency and safety? No marks for guessing the answer to that one. Bye-bye Queeg.

In departing the 3rd Battalion, I was sorry to be leaving behind the many fine NCOs and men who were the very backbone of the Bloods, and I like to think they were also a little sorry to see me go too, but one of us had to leave and it certainly wasn't going to be Con John, which seemed reasonable enough even to me. If you can't beat 'em, leave 'em!

Not all the Bloods officers were that type, I'm glad to say. Jacky Jones, feisty skipper of the barracks soccer team, was always supportive, while the adjutant I recall with great affection and respect.

Con O'Sullivan was a man of extraordinary talents, cultured, well-read and very artistic, and he conducted speech therapy and voice production lessons in addition to organising the musical shows for which the Curragh was rightly famous. But while he never displayed anything but loyal support for those in command, he was also ever ready with helpful advice to any younger subalterns if required.

He could also be tough enough when the occasion required. One morning an irate phone call came through from some senior type demanding that one of the young lieutenants be paraded for calling him a useless bollocks during an argument in the bar the night before.

Con listened respectfully, pointing out the obvious inconsistencies in the accusations against the young man and explaining that, if the caller wished to find redress, the remedy lay in his own hands rather than asking someone else to do his dirty work. The caller finally lost patience with what he saw as Con's prevarication, and ordered him to parade the young man and discipline him immediately - or else!

Con's face flushed with anger. Politely, very politely, he enquired if he was being threatened? The answer was obviously not much to his liking, because he suddenly drew himself up to his full height, held the phone disdainfully out in front of him and, in his most mellifluous tones, loudly bellowed into the earpiece "Sir, kindly FUCK OFF!"

It was a theatrical performance of which even Micheal MacLiammoir would have been proud.

Fourteen
The Depot

The General Training Depot comprised a number of training schools, the biggest of which was the recruit company - recruits from all over the army were sent there to be trained. The others were the Administration and Quarter-Master Wing and the NCO Wing, which turned out young corporals and also prepared senior NCOs for higher rank. The Army School of Physical Education completed the picture.

There was always some course or other taking place, and whenever all the schools were full, the place was a veritable hive of activity. Busy means happy, and I can honestly say that these were the best years of my life in the army. We had plenty of work to do and were allowed to get on with it without hindrance.

Luckily the CO, Pat Dempsey, was a very civilised man, academic and courteous, and Jim Flynn, the adjutant was pretty sound as well, so that working under them was a pleasure. Besides, both hailed from the same area of west Waterford as I did myself, and every now and then we'd hold mournful post-mortems bewailing the fate of our county's hurlers.

They were both very tall men, well over six feet, and had this habit of standing with feet well apart as if to balance themselves, just like a giraffe. One morning at coffee a young subaltern celebrating a promotion, a cheeky sort, approached them both with the offer of a celebratory drink.

"Gentlemen," he announced cheerfully. "The high-balls are on me!" If looks could kill, he'd have been turned to stone.

The depot carried a far greater number of staff than the Bloods, and the officers mess was also much better equipped. A civilian chef, J.B. Flynn, topped up the usual allotment of army cooks, adding just that extra bit of polish to the cuisine, and when shortly afterwards I was appointed mess caterer I quickly came to appreciate his competence and flair.

While much of our food was purchased in bulk at supermarkets and elsewhere, we were always keen to maintain the link which existed between the various messes and the long-established traders in the camp, people like the Farrells, Darlings, Maginns, and the O'Donnells. The O'Donnells in particular were a great boon to me as mess caterer - you could ring them up in a crisis at any time of the day or night, Christmas day or indeed any day, and be sure that Mr. O'Donnell, a gent of the old school, would either deliver the goods himself or dispatch his son Austin to do the necessary. Hard to beat service like that.

One day, a batch of red raw recruits were sent over to the mess to help out while the regular staff were on the range firing their annual rifle practices. A particularly dumb-looking recruit was acting as waiter, under the watchful supervision of the mess sergeant, when suddenly he was requested by one of the diners to fetch some more potatoes. Heading straight for the lift shaft down which all the food from the upstairs kitchen came, the recruit stuck in his head and bawled out at the top of his lungs - "Hey, J.B., more spuds for those hungry fuckers!"

The poor mess sergeant nearly died with embarrassment, and the recruit was swiftly dispatched back over to the recruit lines, while we could clearly hear in the background the sound of J.B's loud guffaws of laughter coming from upstairs in the kitchen. Needless to say the episode raised quite a few titters afterwards in the mess bars.

Training recruits was admittedly sometimes a bit tedious, but it could also be very rewarding. It takes a recruit about eighteen weeks to become a fully-trained or one-star soldier, which includes firing rifle practices on the open range and throwing live grenades. All the grenades kept in stores are covered with a thick layer of grease to prevent rusting, and these have to thoroughly cleaned beforehand to make sure that the springs don't jam and cause the grenades to misfire.

In the event of jams or misfires, the supervising officer, who is installed in a tower overlooking the throwing area, must then descend and detonate the unexploded grenades, having first carefully noted their location. This can be very hazardous.

A young lieutenant lost his life recently as a result of sticking his head up over the parapet without having allowed sufficient time to elapse. As he peeped over the parapet rim to investigate, one of the misfired grenades suddenly exploded and a jagged portion of shrapnel struck him right in the middle of his forehead, directly under the rim of his helmet, killing him instantly.

As soon as the safety pin of a Mills 36 hand-grenade is pulled and the hand-lever is released, you have just seven seconds to get rid of it before it explodes. This can sometimes prove a bit scary because no matter how often recruits practice throwing dummy grenades and no matter how much instruction they're given, the moment they're handed the live grenades and told to pull the pin and throw, they're usually so shit-scared that they just stand there, stuck to the ground and staring at the grenade as the seven seconds ticks away. Sometimes they even drop the grenade on the ground, so terror-stricken do they become.

This is where experienced NCOs are invaluable. They have to judge their actions to the split second and take the grenade off the recruit or pick it off the ground as the case may be, and throw it as far away as they can before it goes off, while at the same time ensuring everyone in the throwing trench takes cover beneath the safety parapet.

While the OC was away in the Congo, command of the GT Depot fell to the Hurler, a gentle giant of a man whose overriding passion was Gaelic football - if a man was a good footballer, he was guaranteed to wear a stripe or even two in Hurler's outfit. This caused some problems, because not all of these guys were up to scratch, while quite a few were downright lazy good-for-nothing wasters. They couldn't be transferred anywhere either because nobody else would have them, so they had to be slotted into cushy jobs in our own unit where they could do the least harm.

The Hurler was also very shy, and nearly died with embarrassment at the Curragh races one day when he went up to a bookie to place a bet on a horse named An Seabhach (The Hawk in Irish).

"Five to two Ann Seeback," roared the bookie, looking around for business, then the Hurler arrived beside him and murmured "I'd like £20 on An Seabhach."

Perplexed, the bookie looked around at his board but failed to identify the horse the Hurler was indicating. Then at last the penny dropped. Turning back to Hurler, he let out a roar which could heard all over the ring.

"Ah, an educated gentleman! Fifty pounds to twenty on An Seabhach, down to the fucking scholar!" And with that he went right back to shouting "Five to two Ann Seeback", leaving the poor Hurler to slink away into the crowd as best he could.

The recruit course normally lasts about eighteen weeks but if, as sometimes happened, a particular recruit wasn't making the grade, he'd be eased out as unsuitable after about six weeks or so. His discharge always had to be backed with reports; reports by the section corporal, by the platoon sergeant, and then by the platoon officer, who'd finally be called before the CO to justify the action.

But poor Hurler's big soft heart made all this normal routine a huge ordeal. He'd hum and haw, heave and sigh, question and prevaricate, and only as a last resort would he grasp the nettle and agree to sign the discharge papers. However, the case of Private Hoban taught him a nasty lesson.

Hoban came from a large family in the midlands and was, to put it mildly, a bit slow. I had already had occasion to send him back from a previous platoon as being unable to measure up, but because the Hurler couldn't make up his mind, he was then foisted onto an inexperienced young second lieutenant to pull him through.

Martin Ambrose, the company sergeant had a soft spot for fellows like Hoban and even punched holes in his target in an effort to pull him through his mandatory range practices, in between dodging the stray bullets and ricochets he sent whistling all around the butts. Strictly speaking, Hoban should never have been sworn in, but the Hurler had felt sorry for him and gave him a chance, saying that a bit of good grub and exercise would make a man of him.

Hoban eventually joined the passing out parade with the rest of the recruits and was then hidden somewhere in the depths of the cookhouse where it was thought he could present the least danger, but sympathy, admirable though it may be, is all well and good provided it doesn't put other people in danger. Wherever guns and ammunition are freely available, you can't afford to mess around and take chances - and sympathy must be chucked out the window.

Poor Hoban must have been terrified out of his wits during his long lonely stints on patrol, all alone out there in the dark among all those concrete bunkers and with the lonely sound of the wind moaning and whining through the telephone wires adding to the discomfort, but he seemed pretty OK as the guard were dismounted and he headed off to spend the rest of the day in bed. Normally eight men shared a billet, and their rifles were securely stacked in the middle of the room in case of emergencies.

About two o'clock next morning, one of the others in the billet awoke to the sound of someone talking loudly on the phone. Opening his eyes, he spotted Hoban cycling a mythical bicycle around the room in the dark, every now and then stopping to ring up a non-existent phone and yelling out at the top of his voice:

"Number one post reporting, sir. All's well."

This carried on for a while, until the whole billet was wide awake and watching. Finally, all appeals to go back to bed having failed, one of the men lost his temper and let fly a boot which hit Hoban a crack on the side of his head. For a moment nothing happened, then he went completely berserk. Roaring like a bull, he rushed to the rifle rack in the centre of the room, unlocked his rifle, and shoved a live round up the breech. Normally every round is accounted for, but somehow Hoban had managed to slip one into his pocket, probably as a souvenir.

I needn't tell you the others hopped out of bed fairly smartly when they heard that rifle being cocked and before too long they had managed to overpower Hoban, though not without a violent struggle. The medical people were then called into

115

action, and Hoban was shortly led away in a straight-jacket for his own safety.

Soon afterwards, the poor fellow was discharged from the army and sent back to his own townland to take up rural work again. Such an idyllic life, free from the stresses and strains of army life, could only be to his best advantage, but whatever about his peace of mind in his rural paradise, no such harmony reigned in the recruit company of the GT Depot. Investigators swarmed through the records like a swarm of angry bees, interviewing all the participants, and soon accusing fingers began to point at those responsible for taking him on.

A quick check revealed that Hoban's family had a history of such conduct which should have automatically rendered him ineligible in the first place. This regulation was only put in place after painful experience had shown that the unusual strains of army life, such as long, lonely patrols and sentry duty, can sometimes tip such a man over the brink.

But now the ripples of suspicion spread ever wider and wider until practically the whole recruit company had been interviewed. Those who had acted correctly, if cruelly, myself included, were exonerated, while others, including poor old Hurler, got their knuckles rapped, in addition to being billed with the cost of Hoban's keep for the period of his service.

That was a costly lesson, especially for such a kind and big-hearted man as the Hurler, who had acted with only the very best of motives in mind. It didn't change him too much, however, because he continued the way he was right to the very top. Good guys sometimes do win.

Fifteen
Orderlies

"The trouble with the army," some wise-arse once said, "is the small officers with the big privates!" Whatever about the truth of that wisecrack, I do know that officers often depended more heavily on some of the experienced enlisted men, 'old sweats', to keep them on the straight and narrow than they'd ever care to admit.

Every officers mess in the army had its own old reliables, each one of them with their own individual characteristics, trusted NCOs and men with long service who eventually came to be looked upon as almost part of the furniture. McKee barracks had 'Peggy' the barman and Larry the waiter, Clarke sported the ubiquitous 'Baldy' Phelan, and Connolly had its very own Charlie Seery.

Up in Cathal Brugha barracks the famous 'Bugler' Walsh held sway, while the Military College boasted of 'Rubber' Nolan and Jock McMarlow, among others. Out in the Air Corps, Mickey Prince seemed to be running the show single-handed, at least as far as games were concerned. The GT Depot also had its fair share of interesting private soldiers, even if none of them ever became quite as famous as the notorious batman in the book 'The Good Soldier Schweik'.

It's a bit of a mystery where the title 'batman' came from, but even today it's still a standard fixture in every wartime battalion battle-order. In battle, a batman's primary job is to look after his officers' welfare while they are off attending to their principal job - organising attack and defence and looking after their men's welfare - but in peacetime it's looked on as a pretty 'cushy' number and nowadays a batman is more commonly known as an 'orderly'.

My own batman/orderly, Pte. Willy Gough, was a quiet, unassuming chap from Wexford who had mastered the technique of slipping in and out of officers' rooms in the early morning hush to polish brasses, boots and Sam Browne belt without disturbing the occupants and was very popular with all ranks. His best mate was Mick Bracken the cook, so when they returned from the Congo loaded with down with lolly, they decided to celebrate the occasion in style. Their first port of call was the barracks canteen where Mrs. Cowley made to serve up their usual pints of beer, but the lads were having none of that.

"Make mine a Remy Martin, Mrs.C," said Willy. "If it's good enough for the officers, it's good enough for us."

They were surprised at how easily the stuff slipped down and the lovely feeling it induced, and from there they took a taxi to the Rising Sun pub in Brownstown to continue the session with some more of their pals. Glass after glass of 'napper tandy' went down the hatch without a bother until the two boys were well and truly 'flutered', and it wasn't too very long after that before they were carted off home to bed, completely out for the count.

But that wasn't the end of the story, not by a long shot. At about five o'clock next morning, Bracken awoke with a start, head pounding, mouth as dry as a badger's arse, his heart hammering wildly in his chest. In a complete panic, he jumped out of bed and let out a scream of terror.

"Jaysus, Willy," he shrieked. "I'm having a heart attack!"

But poor Willy was scarcely in any better condition, and he too ran around the room holding his chest and gasping for breath in a complete panic. By now the whole billet was wide awake, but all the best efforts of their room-mates failed to get the two under control, and when Bracken made a rush for the balcony railings, threw one leg over and attempted to jump, the situation was clearly getting out of hand.

They had to be held down until the ambulance arrived, and then Doc Cahill took one look, had a quick sniff, and took action straight away. It was a strait-jacket job right enough and within minutes our two heroes were being carted off to the hospital security wing, trussed up like chickens ready for the market, to spend the remainder of the night in the clink.

Early the next morning, a call came from the hospital for me to come and rescue Willy Gough and his best mate Mick Bracken. It was all I could do not to laugh out loud at the sight of the pair of them lying there trussed up on the floor of the cell, looking very much the worse for wear and feeling very sorry for themselves, however, there didn't seem too much point in saying anything and anyway I don't think a lecture would have been much appreciated at that juncture. On their release, back up to the depot they went to pick up the pieces once more, but brandy was off the menu for those two for a very long time after that.

Private Kevin Warren, another one of their mates from the GT Depot, was a really good boxer when the army had good boxers, but unfortunately he'd become a little punch-drunk as a result of all the punishment he'd taken in the ring over the years. Occasionally the officers mess would be very hard-pressed for staff due to sickness, leave or whatever, and then, and only then, would Kevin be pressed into service.

It wasn't that Warren was untrustworthy, just that he was a bit of a messer, especially when drunk which was usually every Friday pay-night. His favourite stunt was to bring his scruffy old mutt to the officers mess in the early morning and then to pull the dog's tail outside someone's door to make him bark wildly until he nearly drove everyone insane. He was lucky there, because one crusty old colonel nearly ran him through with his sword one morning after a wild party in the mess the night before.

Every Friday, Kevin's first port of call was the town of Kilcullen where his wife was buried, and from there he'd make a point of visiting every local pub in turn before catching the bus back to barracks. The only problem was that he eventually became barred from all the buses because of his habit of marching up and down the aisle singing rebel songs at the top of his voice, and whenever he did manage to sneak on unnoticed, it wasn't too long before he made such a nuisance of himself that the bus would stop and he'd be ejected and left to totter home on foot on his own. Having endured a few of these late-night hikes back to barracks you'd think he'd have learned to behave himself, but he never did.

He was always having problems with the local police as well, and whenever his case came up in court an officer from our unit would be obliged to go and represent him. This particular day, one such petty charge involved obstructing traffic on the main road in Kilcullen, but Warren tried to convince the judge that there was no basis for the charge whatsoever, maintaining he'd done nothing wrong and the police were just out to get him.

Imagine the scene in court as the Garda sergeant explained how he'd found Warren, drunk as a lord, doing press-ups in the middle of the road at the traffic lights in Kilcullen on the night of the All-Ireland football final, causing traffic jams as far back on either side as Naas and Athy. His biggest task, the sergeant continued, had been trying to restrain angry motorists from lynching him there and then but fortunately the judge, who knew him of old, was in a merciful mood that day and merely gave him a right old tongue-lashing.

It still came as a painful shock when poor Warren was knocked down and killed as he made his way on foot back to barracks late one Friday night, having been duly ejected from the bus for singing and making political speeches. For all his faults, everyone knew and loved Kevin, and the army duly went about the business of making arrangements for his burial by a local undertaker in the family plot in Kilcullen graveyard.

But when his mates in the barracks heard this, they were none too pleased. That wouldn't do at all, they reckoned, no 'fucking civvy' was going to bury their mate if they could help it, so next morning a clatter of picks, shovels, and augurs were drawn from stores and a whole gang headed for Kilcullen graveyard, under the command of the mess corporal, Dickie Sparrow.

All the mess orderlies were there, led by Willy Gough, plus

a contingent from the barracks to lend support; Bracken the cook, Blondie Doyle, McLoughlin the storeman, who suffered from the officer's disease, gout, Billy Fitzpatrick and the mess sergeant, Shem O'Rourke, among them, but first of all they had one important call to make - they had to stop at one of Kevin's favourite watering holes, The Hideout in Kilcullen, if only out of respect. At long last, courtesy call completed, the team headed for the graveyard and since it was such a hot day, a few crates of beer and cider were brought along just in case the work became too thirsty.

It was tough going at first for lads unused to such hard graft but the digging went well enough and soon they had reached a depth of about four feet, when at last the lack of exercise began to tell and the corporal called a rest. They were all lying around, panned out on the grass swigging cider, with Dickie Sparrow down in the hole working away like a beaver, when suddenly the ground gave way beneath him.

CRAAACKKK! His left leg disappeared into a hole in an exposed coffin just below the surface of the earth, where it remained firmly gripped by the jagged edges of the lid. For a moment there was a shocked silence, then Sparrow let out a howl of sheer terror.

"Holy Jaysus, I'm caught!" he screamed. "Gimme a hand up for fuck's sake."

Everyone crowded round the hole, eyes wide with shock, watching in fascinated horror as Sparrow pulled and heaved wildly in an effort to get loose. Suddenly the lid of the coffin came away on his leg, leaving the contents exposed to their view. For one shocked moment nothing happened, then with yells of terror everyone took to their heels across the field, scattering picks, shovels and cider bottles in all directions, leaving the petrified Sparrow to extricate himself from the grave as best he could. Still shrieking in terror, he legged it after them, a piece of the coffin lid still attached to his leg.

It was a muted band who assembled in The Hideout a few minutes later, and proprietor Jim Byrne had to ladle stiff brandies into them to try to calm them down, and by the time Coy. Sgt. Joe Lee arrived post-haste from the Curragh, they were beyond feeling any pain and certainly incapable of digging any further. Ignominiously, alternative arrangements had to be made to have some of those hated 'fucking civvies' come in and finish the grave while the tipsy warriors were ferried back to base.

Next morning, Private Kevin Warren was buried with solemn military ceremonial beside his beloved wife in Kilcullen graveyard, in front of a large crowd of his friends who'd come to mourn his passing. True to form, he'd managed to cause trouble right to the very end, but I like to think he'd get a kick out of that story.

Army courts martial are funny affairs. You can never be sure how things will go, even if the evidence is overwhelming. Army courts takes a more pragmatic, practical view of proceedings, unlike civilian courts where precedential detail and the letter of the law mostly apply. It wasn't at all unusual for an officer to defend a man in a court martial either, because it was a man's privilege to select whosoever he wished to defend him, and if it was a cut and dried case, like AWOL or desertion, why bother to incur lawyer's expenses when the result was more or less guaranteed?

Nowadays, of course, it's not unknown for soldiers to employ high-powered lawyers to defend them in difficult cases, especially those which occur while on overseas service, but back in those days it was much simpler, even though a case would occasionally crop up which would create legal history and attract enormous interest as well. Such a case was Sgt. 'Pop' Hynes.

Pop was employed somewhere in the inner sanctums of Camp HQ and was so efficient and reliable that he was often thought to have more clout than the GOC himself. He knew exactly the inner workings of the system and how things were done, and would often tip people off in advance if they were in hot water.

You could depend on Pop with your life, and so it came as a tremendous shock when he was arrested one day and charged with rustling sheep and selling the meat to the public. People just couldn't believe their ears - it was the only topic of conversation for weeks on end.

He'd been caught red-handed, the story went, himself and a corporal who worked in the abattoir, caught skinning a newly-slaughtered lamb in a disused hut down by the old magazine. It was, apparently, an open and shut case - the only question was how long he'd do in the clink.

The court martial was standing room only, with many more crowded outside. The five officers of the court, complete with medals and ceremonial swords, sat there listening attentively while the prosecution case was read out. Sheep, the prosecuting counsel told the court, had been disappearing from the Curragh for quite a long time past, in fact the situation had got so bad that, to placate the sheep-owners, the military police had mounted a watch on the plains from the water-tower in an attempt to catch the culprits.

Idly scanning the rolling Curragh plains through his binoculars one balmy evening, an alert sentry paid little or no attention to the familiar portly figure of Pop as he strolled slowly along by the side of the isolated old ammunition magazine down near the sports pitch, accompanied by his little Jack Russell terrier, but picture his amazement when he spotted Pop and another man suddenly leap onto a sheep, overpower it and drag it into a nearby hut.

He quickly raised the alarm and a posse of military police was quickly organised, and when they broke down the door of the hut they discovered a sight that took their breath away. The place resembled a miniature abattoir, with legs of mutton and lamb hanging round the walls and the two boys hard at work at a table in the middle busily chopping up a freshly-killed sheep. Pop and his mate were promptly arrested and placed in custody, to await their trial on a charge of sheep rustling.

It looked an open and shut case. The evidence against them was so overwhelming, it seemed, that the only thing left to decide was the scale of punishment. Would Pop lose his rank? Would he go to jail, would he put up any kind of a defence? But, popular opinion went, any defence seemed too preposterous for words, his best course of action was simply to plead guilty and throw himself upon the mercy of the court.

Not a bit of it! Pop, his chubby face a picture of wounded innocence, stood up in the dock, addressed the court, and pleaded 'Not Guilty.' When they had got over their surprise, everyone in the courtroom held their breath while they waited to hear what defence he could possibly offer. You could hear a pin drop as he began to give his evidence.

"I was out for my usual evening stroll, minding my own business," Pop told the court impassively. "When suddenly a sheep attacked me."

For a moment there was a stunned silence, then the packed court rocked with laughter at this unexpected development - even the members of the court martial could barely hide their amusement, burying smiles behind their hands. In the dock, Pop allowed himself a pained smile, then waited patiently till the roars of merriment died down.

"Oh yes, you may laugh," he went on. "It may indeed seem very funny to you, but I can assure you I saw nothing funny at all in being attacked by a wild animal." The courtroom was now hushed, staring in bemusement.

How was he, Pop went on, how was he, a city man born and bred, to know that it was only a sheep and not a mad ram? Again more laughter in court. As luck would have it, Pop went on unperturbed, he just happened to have a knife in his pocket which he used for cutting tobacco and, pulling it out, he stabbed the sheep in self-defence. Another howl of laughter rocked the courtroom.

When the merriment had died down, Pop continued with his evidence. Realising what he'd done, he said, he panicked and decided to hide the evidence. With the assistance of a man who just happened to be passing, he'd dragged the carcass into an empty hut nearby and then decided to dispose of the body by burying it, but since this meant using picks and shovels, which might arouse suspicion, they decided instead to cut it up and dispose of it piecemeal in the incinerators. And this, he announced to the court, was what they were engaged in when the military police broke down the door and arrested them.

A long moment of silence reigned, then a buzz of speculation broke out among the audience. Whatever your opinion, you simply had to admire the brazen nerve of the man, though of course there still seemed no chance of his being acquitted. The courtroom was then cleared while the court went into deliberation.

The cheers which greeted the verdict of 'Not Guilty' could be heard in nearby Brownstown - even the members of the court had smiles on their faces. Delighted supporters chaired Pop out of the building and down to the nearest NCOs mess where celebrations continued late into the night.

There's little doubt that in a civilian court of law he would have certainly 'gone down' for a long stretch, but army courts martial are a law unto themselves and there's no accounting for how individuals will vote. Somehow or other Pop had managed to plant a tiny seed of doubt in the minds of the court and he was entitled to the benefit of that doubt. Nevertheless, the decision to acquit was nothing if not popular, although I have my doubts if the sheep-men would fully agree.

Andy Warhol's remark about everyone being famous for fifteen minutes doesn't, I'm afraid, always apply. Some people seem destined to slide through life without anyone noticing, never making the news, never making waves, never even making a decision if they can possibly avoid it. It's not that they're worthless, it's just that they're shy, unsure of themselves, lacking in confidence, even though in reality they're gentle, decent people who are very well liked indeed if they could only realise it.

Such a man was Mick Cuddy, the depot barber. In reality he wasn't a barber at all but a handyman of sorts, but when the real barber in the recruit company deserted, Cuddy found himself pressed into service and eventually became a regular fixture. Mind you, he was no artist at the game - the majority of the NCOs and men wouldn't let him within an ass's roar of their hair, preferring to let stylish local barber Reggie Darling trim their locks rather than submit themselves to Mick's tender mercies, but since his main customers were mainly raw recruits, any lack of polish didn't matter too much.

Mick had been in the army longer than anyone could remember, all of it spent in the GT Depot, without anyone hardly even noticing. And it would probably have remained that way, except that the men's annual Christmas dinner was coming up and it was tradition that the oldest soldier in the unit would propose a toast to the President as Commander-in-Chief of the armed forces.

As luck would have it, Mick was the Depot's oldest soldier, and as such was selected to make the after-dinner speech. When this decision was announced he completely panicked, but his protests were all in vain. He simply had to make the speech, he was told, tradition demanded it, and so, as the day of the dinner approached, he reluctantly set about learning his lines off by heart.

His big moment would come when the dinner had ended and the cigars and brandy were being served, then he would rise to his feet, and in a loud voice announce, in Irish: "A dhaoine uaisle, An tUachtaran!" (Gentlemen, The President). The attendance would then rise, repeat the toast and drink to the President's health before resuming their seats.

All week long Cuddy went round repeating the phrase over and over again, till at last he had it off pat, but his confidence wasn't helped by his mates teasing him. He'd have to make a speech, they told him, he'd have to welcome the President in person, then afterwards he'd have to sing the national anthem - in Irish! All this was only make-believe, of course, but in the end poor Cuddy didn't know whether he was coming or going.

Early on the day of the dinner he treated himself to a couple of scoops in the privacy of the barber's bunk, just to steady his nerves, then off he headed to the canteen to practice his lines once again, where 'severeal' more scoops followed. By the time the dinner commenced he was well and truly on his ear, seated there importantly at the top table between the chaplain and the CO, and expectation slowly rose as the dinner drew to a close and speech-time approached. Finally, the MC tapped on his glass and called on the most senior soldier to propose the toast.

A hush fell as Cuddy arose and stood there, swaying unsteadily on his feet, eyes blinking like a sheep in a snow-storm. Every eye was on him as he stood, glass in hand, staring straight ahead, his mouth opening and closing like a fish out of water but with no sound coming. A painful silence followed. People stared at him, willing him to speak, but just like Job's wife in the Bible, poor Cuddy was struck dumb.

At long last someone took pity and gave him a gentle nudge, whispering loudly "The toast, Mick, the toast!" This seemed to unlock the blockage. Drawing himself up to his full height, Cuddy steadied himself, took a deep breath, then roared out at the top of his voice:

"A dhaoine uaisle, Arus an Uachtaran!" (The Presidential Palace). Which, to judge from the wild applause, was as good a maiden speech as anyone could ever expect.

Sixteen
The Garret

Every weekend without fail, a whole gang of young officers would head off from the Curragh to Dublin in the hope of breaking the monotony of camp life and staving off frustration and boredom. Some of the more genteel would bunk in at Collins or McKee, where the accommodation and the facilities were more luxurious, but the majority preferred to be put up in Cathal Brugha barracks where most of their friends were stationed.

In olden days Cathal Brugha, named after the 1916 and Civil War patriot, was known as Portobello Barracks, situated right next to Portobello Bridge in the prime location of Rathmines, with its vast acreage of urban flatland and student pubs and haunts.

There was another good reason for its popularity. Hordes of available young females also lived in Rathmines, all of them only too anxious to meet some dashing young army officers who could show them a good time. At weekends the bar would be jam-packed with visitors, all furiously tanking up on cheap booze before heading off en masse to some well-known haunt in the city.

And if the young officers couldn't exactly impress their girlfriends with lavish displays of lolly, at least they came well equipped with oodles of polished spoof which rarely failed to do the trick, then, after a torrid weekend, back they'd disappear inside those imposing iron gates or else vanish somewhere down into the depths of the Curragh, leaving the young ladies in the lurch, only to reappear again at a brand new venue the next weekend.

It was all great fun and largely harmless, but sometimes

providing enough accommodation became a problem. This was solved when Gerry Enright persuaded Jer Costello, the mess sergeant, to improvise a spare billet to handle the overflow. Kerrymen, no matter what their rank, have this special affinity and always look after one another.

Costello was a real character, fond of a jar and with a keen eye for the ladies. Rumour had it he'd been eased out of the Congo by an outraged chaplain who accused him of consorting with a coloured lady of dubious repute to offer the lads some extra 'entertainment', a charge not subsequently proven.

Far from damaging his reputation, however, he was more popular than ever on his return home to Cathal Brugha, and within a very short time this billet became known as 'the garret', the mecca for regular weekenders from the Curragh, plus any strays from other commands. No matter how late the hour, you were always guaranteed a 'doss' in the garret.

Conditions were nothing if not spartan. Rows of hard, narrow iron beds lined each side of the billet, up to twenty at a time. No curtains adorned the windows, no carpet covered the bare wooden floor, no wardrobe or locker softened the garret's harsh institutional impact. The pillows felt like rocks - if you wanted comfort, you brought your own, but this lack of creature comforts never unduly bothered such hardy warriors as Roy Bennett, Christy McNamara, George Staunton, Buzzer Molloy or Martin Cafferty, all fully paid-up members of the Curragh travelling A-team.

Pat Duggan and Des Rooney, two senior captains, were also regular visitors who came up to Dublin to attend the greyhounds in Shelbourne Park every Saturday night. They were always stony-broke afterwards because of an uncanny ability to back losers, and pretty quickly we learned to avoid their hot tips.

Duggan, a dyed-in-the-wool Dubliner, was a man fond of a jar who occasionally suffered from the DTs, but nobody paid too much attention and in any case he was completely harmless. After a feed of booze, he'd just totter into bed and fall fast asleep, muttering incoherently to himself and every now and again shouting out orders to phantom soldiers in his dreams.

Late one night Mick McDonagh, a most affable fellow, arrived back into the garret with two huge black sergeants in tow whom he'd met while competing against the US Airforce in an athletics competition earlier that afternoon. Somehow or other, after a feed of pints, they'd lost their way and were stuck for a place to stay so Mick, feeling sorry for them, invited them back to the garret to spend the night. Too pissed to notice anything, they collapsed into bed and were soon out for the count.

Early next morning, unable to sleep on the unaccustomed rock-hard beds, the two Yanks stood facing a row of urinals halfway down the stone stairs outside the door of the billet, shivering in their singlets in the early dawn cold, when suddenly Pat Duggan appeared groggily between them. Still half-asleep and more than half-plastered, Pat never even noticed them until one of them spoke.

"Jeez, man," one Yank drawled, white teeth chattering in his head. "Dis here's some fuckin' dive, and no mistake."

"Yeah, man, what a fuckin' dump!" replied the other. "Let's git the hell outta here." Then turning to Pat, he drawled in a rich Texan accent "How ya doin', man?"

It took the still-woozy Pat quite a time to figure out that something wasn't quite right, then finally he managed to focus on the two huge black figures standing one on either side of him. Fully convinced that his worst nightmares were coming true, he let out a howl of terror and bolted back up the stairs, leapt into bed and covered up his head, waking up half the billet in the process.

"They're after me, they're after me!" he howled from underneath the blankets. "I'll never touch another drop again in my life, honest I won't."

By now everyone in the billet was wide awake and sitting up in bed, staring in amazement, but then the penny dropped and McDonagh explained what had happened, and everyone just fell around the place laughing - even Pat saw the joke in the end.

Duggan had a chequered career in the army. A handsome

man with a fine brain, he'd distinguished himself with his exploits during the war years but then slowly began to sink downhill as the bottle took a hold.

He'd arrived in the Curragh from Dublin after a hilarious incident during which he was accused of exposing himself in front of the other officers. Far from being a matter of great disgrace, however, this story soon became the subject of great amusement throughout the army though of course I'm sure the brass saw it a bit differently. It happened like this.

Pat, as a company commander in the 2nd Battalion, and knowing that a very important parade was due to take place on the square in Collins Barracks on the following morning, realised he simply had to be on the ball before 0900 hours in order to be ready to lead on his men since he was already under something of a cloud. He therefore left strict instructions to one of his subalterns to call him at 8am on the dot before retiring to the bar, where he got well and truly pickled.

Needless to say, the subaltern forgot all about his instructions and the first Pat was aware was when the brass band struck up right underneath his window, making him jump clean out of bed with the fright. He looked frantically out the window, only to see some of the other companies already preparing to march onto the square.

Dressing himself in a hurry, he just barely managed to get down in time to lead his men out on parade, bottling up his rage as best he could. Parade over, the troops marched away to their lines and then Pat, unable to contain himself any longer, rounded angrily on the young subaltern.

"I thought I told you to call me in time?" he bellowed, purple with rage.

Oh sorry, I completely forgot," spluttered the young lieutenant. "But sure didn't you make it on time anyway."

"Yes, I did," replied Pat. "But look!

And with that he whipped open his long army greatcoat, to reveal himself standing there bollock-naked, all except for his riding boots and cap which he'd barely managed to pull on as he made a mad dash for the parade ground. It took quite a few balls of malt before Pat could be persuaded to see the humour of that situation.

Unfortunately, being transferred to the GT Depot didn't help Pat much and only the incredible loyalty of his company NCOs kept the show on the road. Every morning, the company sergeant would head for the officers mess where he knew his company commander lay in bed, hors de combat, and shortly afterwards he'd return undetected with the boss's signature on whatever documents were absolutely vital to keep the wolves at bay.

Somehow or other those loyal old NCOs managed to shield him so well it became almost impossible to pin him down. Whenever anyone asked about his whereabouts, according to them he'd be on the range, in the gym or carrying out an audit, or doing a course, anything to keep him from prying eyes, and this would last until Pat had finally managed to pull himself out of his current spree, after which he'd resume his capable command until the demons struck again.

Harry Johnson, a brand-new second lieutenant straight out of the college and full of zeal, arrived in the GT Depot in the middle of one of Pat's benders, and after a couple of weeks was surprised that he still hadn't met up with his company commander. Walking down the long mess corridor one day, a bedroom door suddenly opened and a hairy hand shot out and grabbed him shakily by the arm. There in the doorway stood this gaunt figure, clad only in a bulls-wool shirt, hair standing wildly on end, bloodshot eyes staring vacantly at Harry's shiny new Sam Browne. Harry could only gape.

"Who are you?" the figure inquired, with fume-filled breath. Still in a state of shock, Harry assumed that this must be the mess ghost, or else his missing company commander, Captain Pat Duggan.

"I'm 2nd Lt. Johnson, sir," he stammered, trying to pull himself to attention. A long silence followed while Pat took this in, then at last he spoke.

"Orient me, young lad," Pat growled, in a question much quoted in later years. "What fucking day is it?"

To their credit, the army managed to hold on to Pat for another few years until his pension became due, after which he left and little was heard of him for a long time after that. The last known was that he'd died of pneumonia in Manchester, a sad end for such a popular and capable man.

Seventeen
Hollywood Here We Come

One summer's day in 1965, forgetting the old army maxim "Volunteer for fuckall", I volunteered to take a platoon of men up to Ardmore Studios, near Bray in Co. Wicklow, for the making of the film, The Blue Max, starring George Peppard.

Capt. Jack O'Phelan was running the show as army liaison officer, for which we were paid the princely sum of £1 a day, but considering that the civilian extras were earning ten and twenty times that amount, this was really a bum steer. Still, we were all glad to go since it provided an opportunity to get away from the humdrum routine of the camp and see a bit of exciting film action as well.

On arrival at Ardmore, we found hundreds of other army personnel there as well plus some Air Corps pilots, all on big bucks, who were taking part in the aerial dog-fight scenes. Pretty soon we were all allotted either Allied or German army identities and sent to take up various positions in trench-warfare scenes where we were to be strafed and bombed by enemy fighter planes.

I was appointed a German Wehrmacht Ober-Lieutenant and duly swanned around the set in long olive-green overcoat, wearing a cap with slashed peak and a pair of long black leather boots. Leo Hughes, from artillery in Kildare, was also appointed an officer in the Wehrmacht. At first we found it all so exciting, marching around the set shouting out orders and greeting everybody with the Hitler salute, but after a few days lying in a trench in the pouring rain doing the same scene over and over again, all for a miserly pound a day, the novelty soon wore off.

Before very long before we buttonholed Jack to let him

know what we thought of this whole underpaid caper and to his credit he removed the pair of us from the stinking wet trenches and sent us to the sick bay inside the studio itself. Here the make-up people fitted us out with bandages, plaster and crutches, the whole nine yards, and for the rest of the week all we did was loll around the studio, reading papers or telling yarns to pass away the time. It was a scene of the most appalling boredom with nothing at all to break the monotony and, worse still, we never got to see any of the stars even in the distance.

But the nights were magic. When filming finished, we'd collect our pay which had now been increased to £2 a day, and head off for the fleshpots of the city, then it was back to barracks at dawn, just in time to catch the truck for Ardmore where we'd be made up in our hospital disguise once more and lounge around sleepily for the rest of the day.

After a week or two of this, we were totally browned off this film lark and longing for a sleep in a nice soft bed, instead of lying around on a hard floor trying to snatch forty winks. One particular day we had really bad hangovers and were dozing uneasily in a corner when the Gentler shook me grumpily awake.

"Follow me," he beckoned, and led the way out of the studio into a large room off the main corridor, away from all the noise and bustle outside. There in the middle stood a magnificent four-poster double bed, already made up and inviting. We needed no second invitation. Whipping off our greatcoats and bandages, we leapt into bed and before you could say Cock Robin were fast asleep and snoring.

I awoke from my pleasant dreams with the bed being violently shaken. At the foot stood this tall blonde figure, dressed in a German airforce uniform. I thought I vaguely recognised him from somewhere but couldn't quite place him, and he didn't look any too pleased either.

"Who the fuck are you two?" he growled, scowling at us. "And what are you doing in my bed?"

By now the Gentler was also awake and the two of us sat up

in bed, staring blankly at this other German and wondering who on earth he could be, but we were in no great hurry to get out of the bed, assuming, incorrectly of course, that he was just some other chancer like ourselves trying to get in himself.

"And who the fuck might you be?" the Gentler asked, in that soft, polite manner which he always employed when he wanted to unhinge someone. The figure placed his hands on his hips and glared.

"I'm George Peppard, that's who I am, and that's my fucking bed you're sleeping in. I'm supposed to be the star of this fucking film!" We stared blankly.

"And now, " he added with heavy sarcasm. "If you wouldn't mind getting the fuck out of there, I might get in a few hours kip myself, that's of course if you wouldn't mind too much?"

The Gentler and I looked at each other, then decided that discretion was the better part of valour. Hopping out of the bed, we introduced ourselves and explained how we'd come to be there in the first place. At first he said nothing, then he put back his head and laughed and laughed, after which he shook hands, wished us well, then jerked his thumb in the direction of the door.

"Right, out!" he remarked, a hint of a smile on his face, and giving him the Hitler salute, we marched out the door, mightily relieved to be getting off this lightly. I'm bound to say it was most sporting of him to act in this fashion, and I heard that he took great pleasure in relating the tale to his pals later on. George was a real nice guy, with none of that false pride or egotistic behaviour that one often associates with Hollywood movie stars.

The bank strike of 1970 came completely out of the blue, catching the whole country by surprise - shopkeepers, housewives, politicians, publicans, farmers, the lot - and because it was such a surprise, nobody was quite prepared for it. The banks slammed their doors shut before people had a chance to withdraw their money or equip themselves with cheque-books and the like, and the result was almost total chaos.

Since everybody now had to paid by cheque, this caused another problem - where to get enough ready cash to operate? The only people with cash were shopkeepers, hoteliers or publicans, all anxious to unload it in case they were robbed. Pretty quickly the supply of proper cheque books dried up and soon the market was swamped by floods of badly-printed chequebooks printed in all sorts of size and shape, with little or no identifying marks.

And when these chequebooks weren't available, people resorted to using pieces of paper and cardboard, cigarette packets even, with their names and details written on them, in return for cash. As a result, shopkeepers and publicans and the like were highly exposed to being taken for a ride, but there was nothing they could about it - they simply had to cooperate to stay in business.

But while the majority greeted the closure of the banks with horror and dismay, there were those again who thought all their birthdays had come together, such were the opportunities it opened up for 'fiddling'.. Fellows went around wielding bunches of 'bogey' cheque books, and pretty soon businesses were holding large numbers of outstanding cheques in return for things like food, petrol, clothes and the like, with no idea if they were ever likely to be honoured when the banks opened for business again - that is, if they ever did open.

On and on the strike dragged, one month, two months, four months, six - it seemed as if there was no end in sight. In spite of themselves people, even the most cautious, began to relax and get casual about money. They went around buying things they neither wanted nor needed but since these were easily available and might never have to paid for, the attitude was - why not? Let tomorrow look after itself.

Down in the Curragh, things were just as bad if not worse. No one had access to money, cash was like gold dust, and that's what nearly led to my downfall. It happened like this ...

I was secretary of the Derby Ball, run in aid of the Army Benevolent Fund, which event always took place in the new gymnasium on Friday, the eve of the Irish Derby. It so happened that this year it coincided with the Friday that the strike began, and as a result I hadn't been able to lodge the considerable takings from the ball before the banks closed. These amounted to well over three grand, a fair sum in those days, and I urgently required somewhere to keep it safe while the strike lasted, but since no one believed the strike would last longer than a week or two, initially this didn't seem to present much of a problem.

After careful consideration, I decided the best place to hide the loot was in my upstairs bedroom, right in the corner between the wardrobe and the washhand basin where no one would ever be likely to look. I managed to stash the huge bundles of notes and coins in the bottom of an old army kit-box, made of stout seasoned timber and with a heavy Chubb lock securing it, then nailed the box to the floor with six-inch nails, finally wrapping it completely round with coils of heavy chains. This, I reasoned, was the nearest to Fort Knox I could get.

The news quickly spread round the camp that I was the source of a never-ending spring of money and pretty soon a constant queue of punters were lining up to sip at the banquet. Of course I was only too delighted to unload some of that lump of cash in the kit-box, so I regularly handed out wads of notes to lads going on leave, going to the races, going to the dogs, going on foreign holidays, going to funerals, parties, weddings.

If you wanted cash for anything, then I was your kiddo. I'd creep upstairs to my room, glancing stealthily around me like a latter-day Scrooge, undo the chains and unlock the kit-box, and then minutes later return to present the beaming customer with wads of smelly notes of all denominations.

In return, I'd sometimes be presented with a cheque with the bearer's signature and address written on it, but far more likely, late at night in the bar, I'd squirrel away IOWs on filthy pieces of paper or cigarette packets with some illegible signature hastily scrawled across them. I hasten to add that my own name figured prominently among the pile of littered cheques in the box, which, as the strike dragged on, got bigger and bigger by the day till finally there were far more cheques and tattered cigarette packets in the box than cash.

There was no end to my largesse, I appeared to be the most popular man in the whole army but as no end to the strike seemed in view, there didn't appear to be a problem. News bulletins telling of breakdowns in negotiations between the bank authorities and their staff were greeted with whoops of delight, while parties and celebrations gained in momentum as a mood of financial recklessness set in.

People went out and bought cars, houses, caravans, horses even, everyone was dressed up to the nines with the very latest fashions accessories, while holidays to exotic foreign locations really came into their own.

But alas, all good things come to an end, and the bank strike ended just as suddenly as it had commenced. A secret settlement was hammered out late one Friday evening in August, and an announcement was made on the radio and TV news that the banks would be open again for business on the following Monday morning.

To say that this news was greeted with a state of shock throughout the country would be an under-statement. The general public - workers, housewives and such-like - went around in a daze wondering how they could meet their commitments, while the people holding the bulk of the cheques - hoteliers, garages, shopkeepers, small businesses - wondered if they'd ever get paid. It was a terrible time, and as usual the banks didn't give a rattling damn.

Upstairs in my room there reigned a state of complete and utter panic. A quick rummage through the kit-box confirmed my worst fears - most of the cash was gone, replaced by clusters of damp, crumpled cheques and heaps of smelly cigarette packets.

There was even a roll of toilet paper with by now faded illegible signatures on it. Worse still, a quick check revealed that a majority of the IOU owners were either in the Congo, on duty on the border, or else on leave, and, despite a series of frantic phonecalls and telegrams, there was simply no way of contacting them before the Monday morning deadline. Zero hour had arrived.

I went around in a sort of horrified daze, fully aware that if I didn't manage to pull something out of the hat, and quick, I would most likely face a court martial for misusing army funds and possibly be cashiered in disgrace. And while of course I knew that all those who owed me money would pay up in the fullness of time, the very most that I could raise from those of my pals who were still around was in the hundreds, not the thousands that were needed. Besides, a certain amount of secrecy had to be observed in case the army brass higher up might get to hear about it.

There were of course other means of raising the cash. There were always banks to be robbed, as indeed they deserved to be, but alas, the risks involved here were just too much in view of our own security arrangements. I could always resign, but since I was single and didn't qualify for a gratuity, that wasn't much of an option. Moreover, since time was now of the essence, I'd be unable to make contact with those who owed me the money in sufficient time to lodge when the banks opened for business on the following Monday. I wandered around the barracks, sick at heart, and eventually decided to take a trip to the city to get away from the sense of impending doom. Then fate took a hand - sometimes fickle Lady Luck takes pity on a trier.

Walking down Grafton Street, head bowed low and deep in depression, who should I meet but banker Pat Joye, an old friend with whom I'd once soldiered in McAlpine's army on the building sites in London during our student days. Over a pint, I poured out my tale of woe and for once found a ready ear. Luckily for me, Pat had just been promoted from teller to bank manager and was feeling somewhat 'flaithuileach' and anxious to build up his customer base, and I found him very sympathetic to my plight.

The upshot was that at ten o'clock on the following Monday morning I presented myself at Pat's bank and collected a cheque large enough to cover my outlays and more and, within minutes, was burning up the road to the Curragh to lodge the money in the relevant Army Benevolent Fund account to stave off impending disaster.

It had all been a very tight photo-finish, one which had really frightened the bejasus out of me but even now, as news of banking misdemeanours almost daily hit the headlines, I still retain an affectionate regard for banking mavericks such as Pat Joye.

But though the story had a happy ending for me, I can't say the same for Pat. My account followed him wherever he went throughout the remainder of his banking career, which can't have helped him any, but at least he belied the widely-held perception of all bank managers as cold heartless swine.

Eighteen
The Big Smoke

A six-month sojourn in Cathal Brugha Barracks in Dublin made for a pleasant change, when I was detailed to report as an instructor on a potential NCOs course in the Eastern Command. In the past, all the army's potential NCOs were sent to the Curragh to be trained, but now the East decided to do the job themselves with the help of some of the more experienced instructors from the NCO Wing in the Curragh.

The big difference between soldiering in Dublin and the Curragh was the amount of after-hours activities available. In the Curragh, almost all social and sporting activity in the evenings revolved around the camp itself - you were either down on the plains playing games, working out in the gym, or else out on the golf course - but Dublin was a different world altogether.

Every evening on the dot of five, a mad stampede would head out the gate into the bustling metropolis outside. Practically everyone came to work in civvies, changed into uniform once inside, then changed back again in the evening before heading anonymously out into the Big Smoke. Yet, for all their seeming indifference, I was surprised at the professionalism of those eastern soldiers when the chips were really down.

Somewhat to my surprise, I quickly settled into a pleasant routine in my new surroundings. Besides supervising classes and doing the occasional spot of instruction, one of my duties lay in helping my company commander, Capt. Deeney, in supervising the running of the NCO's Mess. Kevin Deeney was an amiable man from Mayo who, besides being an outstanding sportsman, was a dead cool character as well.

Cathal Brugha differed from other barracks in that it contained not one, but two NCO's messes, one for the sergeants and another for the corporals. The old-timer NCO in charge of both, Sgt. Dinny Brannigan, was a born fusser, but very deferential as well. Every second sentence would be prefaced with 'sir', then he'd riddle every other four or five words with 'sirs', which could be very disconcerting indeed. He was also very efficient - far too efficient, Deeney reckoned, who long suspected Dinny of running a 'fiddle' which no-one had been able to uncover despite their best efforts.

The problem was lack of evidence - a good deal of our time was therefore devoted to trying to catch our man in the act, which was much easier said than done. Dinny was a barrack stalwart, a member of the church choir, the trainer of the football team, an organiser of the youth club, and also a trusted confidante of both the CO and the chaplain. Anything that happened in barracks, Dinny had a hand in it, which meant we had to be careful as to how we approached the matter.

Our first job every Saturday morning, was to carry out the weekly inspection of the two NCOs messes, starting first with the sergeants and finishing off with the corporals. On this particular Saturday, Deeney and I marched purposefully down to the NCOs mess, hell-bent on cracking this mystery once and for all, but after conducting a thorough examination of the sergeants mess stock, interspersed with copious cups of tea and biscuits supplied by the eager Dinny, Deeney had to pronounce himself satisfied, we could find nothing wrong. We'd return after coffee break, we announced to Brannigan, and we'd then turn our attention to the corporal's mess.

Half an hour later, we arrived back at the NCOs mess again, to be greeted effusively by Dinny. "Did you enjoy your coffee, sir? And sir, would you like some more tea and biscuits before you check the corporal's mess?"

"Yes, sergeant," Deeney replied. "We certainly did, and we certainly would, but first of all we'll just take another look at the sergeants mess once again, if you don't mind, just to make doubly sure."

At this a look of pure horror came over Brannigan's face, and he collapsed in a heap on the ground, moaning and clutching frantically at his chest. He was clearly an ambulance job and shortly afterwards was carted off to St. Bricin's hospital, to the mournful wail of the ambulance siren, closely attended by the chaplain, Fr. McCabe, who'd arrived puffing. We then turned our attention to the books.

A quick look confirmed our worst suspicions. In order to make up the shortcomings in the stock, the wily Dinny had organised the sergeants' mess for the first of the morning's inspections, which was A-1, then, while we were gone to coffee, he'd wheeled the barrels of beer, cartons of cigarettes, and crates of spirits right across the road to the corporals mess to top up the missing stock in readiness for the second inspection.

Needless to say, no-one had ever tumbled to this stunt before and Dinny had managed to get away with it for years. Mind you, events like this are not unknown in officer's messes either, with many an officer being cashiered over the years for being unable to account for missing mess funds.

The following Monday morning, after a weekend spent celebrating, Kevin Deeney and I received the anticipated call and headed off to the CO's office, confidently expecting to receive his congratulations and to bask in his appreciation. After all, we'd just unmasked a mystery that had baffled people for years. As we came in, I was surprised to notice how grim and unsmiling the CO looked, the chaplain too, but I assumed this was because of their shock at seeing their old friend Dinny unmasked.

But to our complete astonishment, the CO proceeded to give us the father and mother of a bollocking. How dare we, HOW DARE WE treat a loyal and decent soldier like Dinny Brannigan in this manner, pressuring him and putting his life in danger. This was no way to treat a man who'd served the army so well, a man who was the very backbone of the unit. Our actions were simply inexcusable, he growled, and if anything happened to poor Dinny, he would hold us personally responsible.

To say we were stunned would be a bit of an understatement. We could do nothing but stand there and take it, and when the

CO had finished, the chaplain added in his piece - and he didn't mince his words either.

It was a demoralised and subdued pair who finally tottered out of the CO's office and reached the safety of the mess bar, where we took refuge behind a couple of stiff brandies. We sat in in silence for several minutes while Deeney sipped at his drink, then suddenly he began to laugh as the humour of the situation dawned on him.

"Mick, I see now where we went wrong," he chuckled. "We ignored the three golden rules for success in the army."

"And what're those?" I enquired.

"One, volunteer for fuckall. Two, have a good sense of rumour. And three, and most important of all, keep a civil tongue in your CO's hole!"

The position of training officer to the FCA was a much-sought after post, for the simple reason that it got you away from the normal routine of barracks life for a few years and, even more importantly, gave you that extra few pounds through car and travelling allowances. Regrettably I never got a chance to serve with the FCA because I was in an area which at the time had no FCA under its command.

The FCA were sometimes viewed by the regular soldiers as a bit of a nuisance, with their non-stop bitching about the blouson-style 'bumfreezer' jacket and were sometimes sneeringly referred to as Balubas, of Congo tribal fame. And of course it's also true that many only joined in order to qualify for a fortnight's annual holiday in some seaside spot or else to get hold of a stout pair of boots which could be good use either for snagging turnips or for workings on the buildings, which led the force becoming known by the acronym FCA - Free Clothing Association.

We regulars' also liked to take the mickey out of the FCA whenever the opportunity arose. Arriving back in Templemore barracks late one night, I suddenly spotted Frankie Browne from Clonmel FCA, an old drinking pal, marching up and down on sentry duty at the main gate, doing his best to look menacing. On seeing us approach, he unslung his rifle and bayonet and gave challenge.

"Halt!" he yelled, in time-honoured fashion, but before he could complete the challenge I beat him to the punch.

"Who goes there?" I repiled. A long pause followed while he digested this unexpected turn of events.

"I said, Halt!" he bellowed once more, but again I beat him to the draw.

"Who goes there?" I yelled back.

Another long pause followed, then Frankie lowered his rifle and spread his arms wide.

"Ah fuck it lads, hold on a minute," he appealed. "I'm supposed to say that."

For a few moments a stand-off seemed on the cards before suddenly he recognised me and we all fell about the place laughing, but then the corporal of the guard, a regular, arrived at the double and put the lot of us to flight, giving both Frankie and myself, a right old blistering in the process.

But whatever way you looked at them, the reality is that they were dead keen and took the job very seriously indeed, in fact much of the regular's dismissive slagging could be put down to the fact that in many aspects, the FCA often put them to shame. Andy Minihan from Enniscorthy was a colourful high-profile FCA officer beloved of the media, while Mallow's Bill Eager's larger-than-life zeal was perhaps the spur which propelled his sons, Billy and Tony, to later rise to high rank in the regular army.

In every town and village throughout Ireland lay a dedicated cadre of highly-motivated men from every walk of life - teachers, solicitors, craftsmen, labourers, businessmen, farmers - who religiously attended to their duties and set the regulars a very high standard indeed.

In Newbridge, just a stone's throw from the Curragh, printer Larry Bradley was one of the leading lights, while Clonmel's John Burke was another who showed great dedication, in fact

John was among those FCA members called up to the regular army during troubled days in the mid-eighties who then accepted the offer of a regular commission and is now serving as a full-time professional soldier in Kickham Barracks.

In my own town, health board official George Glanville and businessman Richie Keating were the local officers who set the pace, ably assisted by postman Seamus O'Brien who was one of my mentors during my boy scout days, while creamery worker Michael Power and barber Mick Cashman were among the outstanding crack-shots rifleman of the southern force.

And in the cities, several elite artillery and cavalry units existed which would not have disgraced themselves in any army. In McKee barracks in Dublin, these were led by stalwarts like Joe Gallagher who willingly gave their time and energy towards producing a back-up reserve of well-trained personnel which could be called upon to supplement the regular army in times of emergency.

It was perhaps fitting that their professionalism and selfless dedication eventually gained their just rewards during the dark and dangerous days of the Northern troubles when many of the state institutions were under threat and the army was under such pressure what with all-encompassing security duties in addition to overseas UN service. Beside being issued with decent weaponry such as the FN rifle, the Gustaf SMG and the Fn pistol, they also got their wish at last and were issued with a proper full-length tunic, bringing them more into line with the regular army.

And with the regular army's resources stretched to the absolute limit with security duties such as Portlaoise and the Curragh prisons, guarding government buildings and other sensitive areas, in addition to providing protection for cash convoys to banks plus providing enough troops to fulfil our commitments to the UN overseas, it was then that the FCA really came into its own.

They provided back-up for regular troops at sensitive moments and also filled the onerous task of guarding army barracks, government buildings and key power installations which were under constant threat by subversives, thereby affording the hard-pressed regular troops some relief. As one high-ranking general put it: "Without the FCA, we simply couldn't have managed."

Nineteen
Harry Agony

Throughout our lives, people come and go, slipping in and out of our consciousness with equal facility. Some of them we remember with no great affection as ogres of the past, posturing little Hitlers who manage to make people's lives a misery, while yet the mere mention of another man's name evokes a spontaneous smile, recalling all their joie de vivre, their essential mischievousness.

Such a man was Harry Agnew, or 'Harry Agony' as he was affectionately known, one of the best-known and best-loved characters in the Eastern Command. Harry was a garrulous, roly-poly, happy-go-lucky sort of fellow, fond of drinking, carousing and gambling, an amiable, lovable, cheerful hedonist who laughed his way through life and gathered few if any enemies along the way. Realising the fun to be had, I quickly attached myself to his travelling team while in Dublin.

Way back during Emergency days, in an earlier incarnation in the army, someone had put Harry into the same boxing ring as a fellow called O Colmain and instructed him to have a go. This guy's a big bag of shite, his second advised him, tongue in cheek, just put him under pressure and he'll collapse like a stuck balloon, but what he didn't tell Harry was that his opponent was none other than Gearoid O Colmain, who was afterwards European heavyweight champion.

Taking him at his word, at the sound of the bell Harry rocketed across the ring and showered a veritable avalanche of punches from all directions on O Colmain, who was hard put to defend himself against this unexpected onslaught. As he sat down on his stool at the end of the round, he was heard to anxiously enquire of his second: "Who is this fucking guy anyway?"

But then, halfway through the second round, Harry ran completely out of steam, and a well-chosen left hook from O Colmain put him flat on his arse in the middle of the ring. This may have earned him a standing count from the referee, but it also earned him a standing ovation from the crowd as well. People everywhere admire a brave man.

Everyone thought the world of Harry - everyone except his bank manager, that is! Like many a swashbuckler fond of the good life - and the army always had plenty of those - he had a wonderful penchant for spending money, and in those cash-straitened days it was a mystery how he'd managed to survive at all without the bailiff baying at his heels. Hardly a party or dogfight was held that he didn't attend; as far as Harry was concerned, good fortune was waiting around the corner, gloom was for the depressed, so cheer up, folks, let's live it up!

So when he was selected to go to the Congo, Harry's joy knew no bounds. Goodbye at last to all those penny-pinching years, farewell to penury and frugality, welcome the good life once again. The devil, it seemed, was definitely looking after his own.

A series of parties was quickly arranged to which all his friends were invited, and of course his bank manager too - his delight was, if anything, greatest of all at the thought of the unexpected financial windfall about to fall into his lap. As usual, Harry was the life and soul of the party, singing and dancing till the wee small hours without showing the slightest sign of fatigue.

His arrival in the Congo made no difference to his lifestyle. Almost every night there'd be a party somewhere, all of which Harry would attend, and very soon he became a byword among all those sober Scandinavian types who'd never come across anything like him before in their lives. They hung on his every word, and he had no shortage of those, and followed him slavishly around in a posse from party to party.

Then Harry got his knuckles shot off in a trench during a skirmish with the Katangese militia and after only a short few weeks in hospital, was on his way back home to Ireland to convalesce. When the news of his departure broke, with a likelihood that he'd never return, a deep gloom settled on the UN contingent. Farewell parties were attended in droves by all the various nationalities, each heartbroken at the prospect of Harry's imminent departure.

The entire Congo adventure ended shortly after that, but then Enosis broke out in Cyprus and once again Harry found himself heading overseas bound for that Mediterranean Isle of Love, once again after the usual round of farewell parties. His bank manager, needless to say, was overjoyed at the news.

But if the Congo was enjoyable, Cyprus was sheer heaven. British occupation meant that a large proportion of the population spoke English, which made socialising less difficult, and a constant stream of tourists, many of them Irish, provided a fertile source of entertainment heaven-made for someone of Harry's talents. He soon set a cracking pace.

Night after night the show rolled on, sometimes in the Irish mess, sometimes in a foreign contingent's camp, or again in one of the many watering holes which dotted the island and leading the assault was Harry, who rarely sallied forth without a multi-national entourage in tow.

On his way back to base one evening, after a particularly difficult day spent patrolling some trouble spots in the hot Mediterranean sun, Harry parked his white UN jeep by the side of a bar while he slaked his thirst with a cool ouzo. The short break became an extended one till finally it was time to head for base, but by now the sudden tropical night had fallen.

To his driver's dismay, Harry insisted on driving, and off they headed in the approximate direction of home. Trying to negotiate the maze of narrow streets and alleyways by daylight was bad enough, but in the dark it was an absolute nightmare, and pretty soon they were completely lost in an area which was out of bounds to all UN personnel.

As luck would have it, their somewhat erratic passage in the white-painted jeep was shortly afterwards picked up by alert UN patrol cars, manned by Finnish military police, who quickly settled in behind Harry's jeep and signalled vigorously for him to pull over.

Harry pull over? You must be joking! Down went the boot and away went the chase, Harry in the lead, chased by a growing convoy of UN jeeps, lights flashing, horns blaring madly. Down winding narrow alleys, up steep cobbled hills, across smooth tarmac boulevards shot the noisy caravan, the lead jeep twisting and sliding in all directions, brakes screeching in a desperate attempt to shake off its determined pursuers in a scene straight out of the Pink Panther.

At last, hemmed in on every side and with all escape routes cut off, Harry searched desperately for a way out, and was on the point of surrendering when suddenly he spotted a large entrance with ornate wrought-iron gates ajar which seemed to offer a safe haven from his pursuers. In he swung and accelerated as fast as he could up the driveway, but the flotilla of UN jeeps gave chase and managed to jam him at a junction, cutting him off - they had him at last!

But they reckoned without Harry. Revving furiously, he plunged the jeep across a huge flower-bed in the direction of the entrance, but after only a short distance it got bogged down in the soft newly-watered earth. Engine screaming at maximum revs, the jeep slewed violently all over the garden, wheels spinning wildly, sending plants, flowers and shrubs flying in all directions.

Finally it stopped dead, unable to make any further progress, and the UN police closed in for the kill, assisted by the trigger-happy guards of Cypriot President Makarios, whose garden it turned out to be. Even for Harry, this meant big trouble. Makarios was reported to be furious, while the UN head bods in New York nearly went berserk. Back at Cyprus UNIFIL HQ, confusion reigned, with the wires between the embarrassed Irish contingent and army HQ back in Dublin humming briskly.

At last the fateful decision was reluctantly taken - they were sorry, but Harry just had to go. A few days and a few riotous farewell parties later, Harry departed Cyprus for Erin's green shores, to the deep regret of the entire UN contingent and a lot of the Cypriots as well, who had all fallen under the spell of this rumbustious, irreverent, devil-may-care Irishman who had briefly brightened their lives.

Some say his bank manager finally threw in the towel after that, but somehow I doubt it. I suspect he secretly admired Harry and would have hated to see a man of his calibre going down the tubes if he could possibly help it.

Strangely enough, it didn't do him any great harm in the army either. Back home again, he quickly settled into his old routine as if nothing had ever happened, and the Makarios story gained legendary proportions in mess bars down through the years. After all, it's not everyone manages to mess up a President's garden and lives to tell the tale.

Harry was a big man, big-minded, big-hearted; perhaps that's why nobody ever managed to put him down. I guess it's universally true that people everywhere admire a man with balls - and Harry Agony had those in abundance.

Twenty
Mrs. Keaveney

The famous columnist and raconteur, Myles na gCoppaleen, once remarked of a particular type of extreme Irishman : "You may meet an ordinary, civilised, decent-looking man, but scratch beneath the surface, and he'll produce his handball medals."

I have that same funny feeling about westerners. You can socialise with them, play games with them, even stand for their children, but share a few drinks too many and you'll soon see the real man emerge, and a wild one at that. Maybe it's the poitin.

I never served in any Western Command unit, which is maybe just as well - but what a strange bunch they were. Athlone town houses the main bulk of the west's troops, while Mullingar harbours mainly artillery, which includes mortars and anti-tank. The most western outpost is the 1st Battalion based in Galway, known as An Cead Cath because it's the only Irish-speaking battalion in the army.

One of the best-known soldiers in the Cead Cath was Seamus O Coinghealaigh, who hailed from Spiddal and could speak no English. When on leave, Seamus was in the habit of dropping in regularly for a drink to a local pub owned by a lady named Mrs. Keaveney. Eventually he left the army and went off to work in England, and on his first visit home for Christmas was enjoying a quiet drink in the bar when the land-lady engaged him in conversation.

"Tell me, Seamus, are you home for long?" she asked. "And how do you like it over in England?" But to each and every question his answer was always the same.

"Fucking sure mate, Mrs. Keaveney!" he'd reply without a blink, reflecting the tiny amount of English he'd picked up on the building sites and in the pubs thall i Sasana. To this day, that cant is still very popular in An Cead Cath.

Once or twice a year, Southern Command would have to make a trip west to play them in rugby, gaelic, hurling or soccer. Invariably these would be tough affairs, because no matter whether they had a good team or not, they'd fight like tigers and you'd be lucky to escape with your life. This particular year, Southern Command dispatched what we considered to be a really good team to play the West in the final of the all-army rugby competition in Athlone.

We were confident that our team, which included some top club players and a couple of inter-provincials, among them Gerry Kenny who scored that famous try for Munster against the All-Blacks, would give them a real thrashing, even though they also had a few experienced players like Terry O'Neill, Paddy Keogh and John Corrigan.

I was modelling on one wing, Sean Berry from Bohemians on the other, leaving all the gouging and boring to our big forwards who seemed to enjoy it all hugely. Pretty soon the game dissolved into a brutal brawl between the rival packs - army games were notorious for their lack of mercy. The game was nearing its end, with the South cruising comfortably home and me congratulating myself for not even getting my togs dirty, when suddenly their out-half lofted a despairing Garryowen high in the air which slowly sailed in my direction.

I positioned myself to make a mark, keen to avoid the mad onward rush of Crazy Horse, in the form of Mick Tallon, all six feet four of him, blazing blue eyes topped by a fiery red mop and a ferocious temper, bearing down fast on me from about five yards away. Although under some pressure, I made the catch and neatly stepped into touch - better be safe than sorry.

I woke up on the sideline ten minutes later, still poleaxed, stars dancing in front of my eyes from the late tackle which rattled every tooth in my head and left a long sliver of lower lip dangling down over my chin. Mick of course vehemently denied any foul play, maintaining he had merely committed himself fully to the tackle and was unable to pull up in time.

Whatever about the rights and wrongs of that, Tallon himself got carted off in the ambulance shortly afterwards, the result of a thorough gouging from lock Gerry Healey, who conveniently blamed poor eyesight for some of his more notorious efforts.

This of course was of little consolation to me but you can't hold grudges, and later on I got to be kind of fond of Crazy Horse, who was a real true-blue even if he did have a short fuse. I first met him during our interview for cadetships as he confidently assured us greenhorns that, unlike us dummies up from Waterford, he'd found the interview an absolute doddle and he'd be seeing us all shortly on the Curragh.

He did see us on the Curragh, alright. As the three cadet classes marched down to Sunday mass in the old pontoon garrison church, hundreds of raw recruits were drawn up on the depot square waiting their turn to march and there, right in the middle of them, was Crazy Horse, green forage cap stuck on top of shorn red locks, sticking up from the surrounding bunch like a furze bush in a gap. He hadn't allowed his failure to gain a cadetship to sap his confidence but had pluckily joined up in the Cead Cath as a recruit and then succeeded in gaining a cadetship the following year. That's determination for you.

The rugby match over, we all retired to the bar to swap reminiscences and have a good laugh over a few drinks, a practice which ensured nobody harboured a grudge from the day's battles - if you felt sore about something, you had it out there and then. Afterwards, to wind up a perfect day, everyone headed to a disco out town, having first ensured that our minibus driver was happy with the decision. For his part, he seemed delighted to be coming along, but our pleasant trip had a nasty sting in the tail.

On the way home, it soon became obvious that the driver was operating none too efficiently. At times the minibus swerved alarmingly all over the road, once going right up on the ditch at a corner and throwing sleeping bodies out onto the floor.

At first I remonstrated with him, but to little effect. Finally, after one particularly hair-raising incident which saw us just barely miss an oncoming truck, I felt I had to take action and warned him about his careless driving. At this he suddenly lost his temper and leapt out of the car, running away down the road and leaving the rest of us sitting there helplessly in the dark.

As luck would have it, two of the party were from the driver's own unit, the Supply and Transport corps, and they did their best to try to settle the matter so that we could all get home to bed. Groggy and all as they were, they attempted to cajole him back into the vehicle but he still refused, saying I had unfairly criticised his driving and demanding an apology.

I knew he'd been drinking, but naturally couldn't be sure if he was drunk or not. It was a very sticky position, with everybody tired and anxious to be at home; he of course realised this as well but was determined to take advantage of our plight. Now a heated argument took place right there in the middle of the road, with the two S&T officers maintaining that he was their responsibility, and me insisting that, as the most senior officer present, it was my decision.

All this might seem rather silly, but I was acutely aware that in the case of an accident these matters could be of great significance and it was my neck, not theirs, that would be on the block. In addition, since there were some cadets aboard, this wasn't the most edifying scene for them to behold, and besides, I had no intention of being court-martialled over some thick northerner's petty fit of pique.

Over-ruling the others, I surveyed the situation. I had two options: one was to put the driver under arrest and send for a replacement driver either to Athlone or the Curragh, which could take hours and risk getting home sometime after daylight which was bound to spark an inquiry.

I chose the second. He was ordered back into the cab and told to resume driving under the direct control of the two S&T officers, but he then went into a sulk, threw his keys on the ground and refused to budge. Things were getting past a joke. At last, after more heated exchanges, the S&T officers took him aside and managed to persuade him to resume the journey, and we then proceeded on our way without further incident. On arrival at the Curragh at dawn, we reported to the Military College to drop off the cadets, whereupon I promptly placed the driver under arrest.

Next day, after consulting his unit adjutant, I decided to be lenient and only charge him with the lesser offense of careless driving, punishable by a fine, instead of the more serious charges of refusing to obey a lawful order and of abandoning his vehicle, which were court martial offenses. But you learn the hard way - sometimes it's better to give certain people the full lash rather than try to be merciful, which all too often they interpret as a sign of weakness.

Arraigned before his own CO, the driver was found guilty of careless driving and fined the nominal sum of £1, but he refused to accept the punishment, as was his right, and opted for court martial instead. Now it began to dawn on the two S&T officers how foolish they had been in their leniency, because this man had a record of such behaviour and would go for the jugular if he could.

He chose as his defending counsel an ex-cadet school officer, a real 'bad bastard' who'd left the army under a cloud and still had a massive chip on his shoulder. He obviously decided this was an ideal opportunity to exact revenge because he tried his level best not just to get his client off on the careless driving charge but to nail all those in the minibus to the cross as well.

We were, he told the court, a disgrace to our uniforms, a drunken, indisciplined, loutish bunch not fit to hold a commission. Coming from someone like him, I thought that really rich. The driver was then called, whereupon he spun some incredible yarn about how he had been driving his vehicle in a careful and thorough manner, as was his wont, but had been repeatedly hampered by drunken and raucous passengers, myself included. It was an unbelievable performance.

Suddenly, from being a simple trial of our driver, the situation was now that we were virtually on trial ourselves for drunkenness and behaviour to the prejudice of good order and military discipline, a serious offense for any officer. It quickly became clear that the defence counsel, with the full encouragement of the driver, was set to do his level best not just to exonerate his client, but to put us into the dock instead.

However, he wasn't as smart as he thought. Calling the barman from the officers mess in Athlone to testify was, he reasoned, a master stroke which would finally put us on the deck, but he reckoned without the fact that one of the officers on board had taken no drink at all - me. At the time, I was preparing for a major athletics competition and had drunk only minerals all through the session in Athlone, a fact which the barman was only too happy to corroborate.

At this both their faces fell, and the case was shortly afterwards wrapped up with a conviction by the court and, better still, an increased punishment of 21 days in the Glasshouse against the driver. It was all I could do to resist giving the pair of them the 'Harvey Smiths' on our way out of court.

Fucking sure mate, Mrs. Keaveney!

Twenty One
The Tin of Beans

Unlike many another job, you could never say that army life lacked variety - the nature of the activities saw to that. Square pegs were made to fit into round holes and people found themselves appointed to jobs to which they were totally unsuited, for no other good reason than they were the only ones available at the time. But there wasn't anything much to be done about it, you just had to grin and bear it.

I must admit to getting a hell of a shock myself when, fresh from an intensive nine-month-long Command and Staff course in the Military College, I found myself posted as adjutant of the field hospital unit of the Curragh military hospital. Just what use my new-found expertise in psy/ops, divisional planning and operational strategy would be in this new appointment was never fully explained, and my introduction left me more puzzled than ever.

I found out later that the real reason I was sent to the hospital was because the men had staged a protest during the annual Command OCs inspection by leaving piles of rubbish in the middle of the billets instead of having them spick and span as expected, and the astute Jimmy Quinn, instead of losing the head as others would have done, realised that something was definitely rotten in the State of Denmark and decided to send in the first available person to sort out the mess - which just happened to be me.

As I was later to discover, the men really had something to protest about. They were being short-changed over rations - most of the married personnel who were in receipt of marriage allowances were illegally dining at their expense every day -

but they were also being screwed in other ways, a situation which took me quite a while to sort out but that's a story for another day.

I was walking down the red-linoed corridor linking the wards on my very first day in the hospital when suddenly I spotted a noisy group coming towards me, arguing loudly, led by a huge barrel of a man weighing at least twenty-two stone. A small head with no apparent neck seemed to be jammed on top of his gargantuan bulk but he still moved at an astonishing rate for such a big man, a sort of crab-like shuffle which made the rest of them almost run to keep up.

Large twinkling baby-blue eyes were set in a soft, moon-like face, with several chins hanging below and a fringe of jet-black hair topping the lot, and he exuded an air of almost childlike innocence, a hidden mischievous exuberance just waiting to burst forth on the slightest provocation. When amused, he emitted a loud high-pitched laugh which just exploded from his hefty frame, putting one in mind of the squeal of a bull elephant.

A copy of The Sporting Life was tucked underneath one arm, the Irish Field under the other, and he kept waving his arms about wildly as if to swat away so many annoying mosquitoes. Spotting me, he suddenly slowed to a halt and spread his arms wide. For one awful moment I thought he was going to embrace me, and hurriedly stepped back a pace or two.

"Do you see what I have to put up with?" he roared, eyes popping out of his head with indignation. "They want me to sign all these forms, and in duplicate and triplicate too."

"But, sir," chorused the pack plaintively, crowding in on him from every direction, sheaves of forms clutched in their out-stretched hands. "We've been waiting for ages for you to show up. You promised you'd sign them last week, and if they're not in by this afternoon, we'll all be in trouble."

The big man stopped and stared at them, a pained expression on his face."Don't you know what's on today?" he demanded. "Punchestown's on, that's what, and there's no way I'm missing the races just to sign any bloody papers. You can wait till tomorrow."

And with that he wheeled into the nearest nurse's bunk, levered his huge bulk awkwardly out the window, watched by the astonished nurses, then disappeared at a fast trot in the direction of the main gate, leaving the crestfallen pack milling around outside the bunk door. Apparently this wasn't a new experience for them because, after waiting for a while, off they headed down the corridor and out of sight, muttering to themselves and shrugging hopeless shoulders of resignation as they went.

Such was my first meeting with Des Rooney, hospital quartermaster, gambler, doggie man, form book expert, epicurean, practical joker and all-round raconteur, who was destined to have a profoundly adverse effect on my career but who was also to provide me with the greatest amount of laughs I have ever enjoyed in my life.

Mind you, he also landed me in an awful lot of hot water and severely damaged my credit rating as well, but that was a small price to pay for being the close confidante of probably the greatest character the army has ever known. Big Des Rooney was a larger-than-life figure in every sense of the word.

Des just loved his cushy job in the hospital and seemed to know everyone, from nurses, to wards-maids, to doctors, to cooks, and they in turn knew and loved him. Every one of them recognised what a warm, lovable man at heart he really was, a harmless, mischievous Billy Bunter look-alike, even if his workrate was sometimes a bit below par.

For years past he'd lived all by himself in the run-down medical officers mess across the way from the main hospital building, where he kept his greyhounds and read his form books and was as happy as a pig in manure, but his lone occupancy was disturbed by the arrival of Willie Dunne and a new doctor, Claude Carroll, followed shortly afterwards by myself and dentist Tom McNally, which soon filled the small mess to overflow.

Because it had fewer people living in, the medical mess was

fortunate if it got a lick of paint every twenty years, never mind seven, but to our surprise and delight, one day an army of decorators arrived, complete with ladders, buckets and paint, and within a few short weeks the place was transformed.

The ante-room was an absolute gem. The ceilings and edges were painted a delicate cream, while the walls were covered in expensive flocked paper, featuring a gold-embossed motif on a dark maroon background. Damask rose curtains completed the ensemble, set off by state of the art furniture straight from the classiest showrooms. The piece-de-resistance was the magnificent carpet, a rich wine shade with tiny floral patterns and a deep pile that you could sink to your ankles in.

Des just loved to wallow in the plush comfort of the place, sprawled in his favourite extra-large couch placed right in front of the fire. Col. Cyril Joyce, the CO, was also as proud as punch - at long last he was in a position to invite friends and colleagues to his mess without feeling ashamed.

With Big Des in mind, strict rules were drawn up to ensure that the mess would be kept up to scratch - after all, it might be another twenty years or more before it got another face-lift. Like many a gambler, neatness and personal hygiene weren't terribly high on his list of priorities but now he was on his best behaviour, taking his nocturnal snacks in the kitchen and keeping his favourite greyhound out the back rather than bringing it in to share the leftovers.

One night, after he'd again lost his 'marbles' at the dogs, severe lack of funds reduced him to a miserly takeaway chicken and chips, which he then brought back to the mess to share with the nurses, who travelled more to enjoy his company than for a love of gambling. Des was the possessor of an almost insatiable appetite which accounted for his enormous bulk.

Feeling a little peckish one day, he dispatched his orderly out town for two chickens and five bags of chips, enough for four men but in his eyes a mere morsel barely enough to keep the wolf from the door. At dinner, you could barely see his head behind the mound of potato skins heaped high on his plate.

In the kitchen, Chris Hegarty and Eileen Foley from the

Families Wing were slaving away preparing the grub on the hot range, helped by Nancy Corrigan, while Des toddled off to heat some beans over the ante-room fire. The Families was a great favourite with late night-owls who made a habit of calling there on the way home. Of course their company also helped the nurses pass away the long night, and many a romantic attachment resulted from such unlikely occasions.

In his haste to heat the beans, Des scarcely noticed Willy Dunne sitting there hunched over the blazing turf, deep in the Irish Times crossword. Willy, fully absorbed, paid no attention to Des either as he reached over him and gingerly placed the large unopened tin of beans on the hearth beside the glowing flames, and there it lay, like a ticking time-bomb, while Des babbled on about some nonsense or other.

BANG! Suddenly the Times disappeared from Willy's grasp, whistled up in the air and stuck to the roof of the ceiling, glued there by an evil-smelling mixture of baked beans and turf dust as the unopened tin exploded. A choking cloud of smoke and ashes billowed out from the fireplace, causing the pair of them to run blindly from the room, wheezing and coughing like refugees from an old folk's home.

Shocked, we all came running when we heard the commotion, but were beaten back by the fumes. Flaming bits of turf littered the furniture and the floor and before you could say Jack Robinson, the new curtains and carpet were ablaze. It was clearly a job for the fire brigade, and within minutes platoons of men in oilskins were trooping through the place, spraying water everywhere and dragging dripping hoses from room to room in an effort to quench the blaze.

When they had finished, the newly-decorated mess was a complete disaster. Cyril's pride and joy was reduced to a damp, smelly, dirty shambles. Murky water ran in filthy rivulets out into the street, while evil-smelling clouds of smoke and steam clogged the air for days afterwards. A council of war was hastily convened around the kitchen table, in a desperate attempt to see what could be salvaged from the disaster. Des was almost beside himself with panic.

"Oh Jaysus, Cyril Joyce will go mad when he sees the place," he moaned. "And I'll be odds-on to get my ticket."

At this we all laughed out loud, but it was apparent that some kind of damage limitation was required, and quickly, so when Cyril arrived next morning to be confronted with the disaster scene, Des was quickly at hand with an official engineer's report to explain what had happened. An electrical fault was the culprit, the report read, and only for prompt actions on the part of Capt. Rooney and his companions, the entire hospital might well have gone up in flames.

Des even managed to look embarrassed while Cyril congratulated him on his quick actions, but nobody ever breathed a word and the truth remained hidden. The mess was patched up again shortly after that but, good though it was, it never again quite reached its previous voluptuous standards. Nighttime catering, and particularly unopened cans of beans, were off the menu forever after that.

The head chaplain was a more remote figure than the other two chaplains, Fr. Colm and Fr. Lar, and also somewhat pompous, so when all the tally-ho over IRA prisoners on hunger strike in the military hospital erupted, he was in his very element. No decision could be made without consulting him. He particularly loved handling the media and being at the centre of all the action, since he fancied his skill in giving interviews and adored seeing his name in the papers and on TV.

But this high profile attracted a lot of criticism as well, particularly from the soldiers guarding the hunger strikers, who objected strenuously to the striker's leader being given Communion twice a day instead of the usual once.

The security unit commander, Captain Mick O'Dea, a prickly Kerryman, was especially upset, though I suspect the real reason was because he'd been bested by the reverend in an argument at table one day and Kerrymen are notoriously slow to forget such slights. As the rumblings and grumblings continued, O'Dea's temper boiled over, and he issued the chaplain with an ultimatum.

"If the present arrangements of twice-a-day Communion continues," he threatened. "I'm going to march my men up to the local Protestant church next Sunday."

This fairly set the cat among the pigeons. Freddie Knowles, the rector, tried to talk him out of it, but to no avail. Freddie was a true-blue Dub with an accent which wouldn't have disgraced Croke Park's Hill 16, and was very popular with the troops. A series of frantic messages and phone-calls flew between the hospital and Army HQ, and between Army HQ and the chaplain's residence, and repeated demands by the head chaplain for O'Dea to be recalled to Cork were received - but he wasn't going to be intimidated as easily as all that.

Arraigned before the powers-that-be, O'Dea defended himself by stating that it was totally unreasonable to expect his men to receive Communion only once a day while a terrorist hunger-striker was allowed to take it twice - there could be no backing down on this.

No betting who was going to win this argument, though it did take a while to settle. The eventual outcome was that O'Dea stayed put, and the issue of Communion for hunger-strikers soon resumed the normal allotment.

The head chaplain lost that round.

Twenty Two
The Rosary Rally

We've all heard stories about weird and wonderful alternative medicines and heard medical experts denounce practitioners as quacks and, worse, fakes and scoundrels, and I admit to having subscribed to such views myself until I witnessed a demonstration which completely changed my mind.

While at a conference one afternoon, the meeting was interrupted by the most awful shrieks and roars coming from the direction of the hospital corridor. Running outside, I witnessed a man being carried on a stretcher towards the operating theatre, being restrained by several orderlies as he writhed and twisted in agony, his screams of pain filling the air and lifting the hairs on the back of the head. It seems he'd been injured in an explosion in the Glen of Imaal in which both his knees had been badly shattered, with bits of bone plainly visible through his tattered trousers.

Suddenly a small, slight figure appeared and signalled to the orderlies to place the stretcher on the floor. He pulled a gold watch from his pocket, held it out in front of him swinging from side to side, then commanded the injured man to watch it, all the while murmuring over and over in a soft, soothing voice ... "Relax, relax, you will feel no pain, you will feel no pain ..."

At first I thought the man was mad but then watched in amazement as the writhing figure on the stretcher relaxed and ceased roaring, whereupon the orderlies carried him to the theatre where the hypnotist, Dr. Gibson from Naas, set his knees in plaster without as much as a whimper from the patient, who was conscious and watching the whole time. Seeing is believing.

For all its lack of real soldiering, the military hospital had some really weird and fantastic characters, most of them doctors. Besides the CO and his second-in-command Badger Burke, who spent most of their time either drinking in the bar or plotting one another's downfall, there was Tony Cahill, multi-faceted and genial, and Henry O'Shea, who enjoyed nothing more than taking on the professionals on the shooting range and beating them.

But of course the NCOs ranks contained quite a few oddballs as well. One such was Sgt. Tommy Tracy, the medical corps Walter Mitty, a multi-talented man with a smooth line of patter who could almost convince people that Hitler was a pacifist.

A typical jack-of-all-trades and master-of-none, Tommy had this uncanny ability to pick up high-falutin medical gobbledegook without having a clue what it all really meant, and was then able to convince anyone gullible enough to listen that he had extensively mastered the subject. Placing him properly in the unit was a real problem.

He'd already been given the boot from the operating theatre for attempting to carry out minor operations on some of his pals, while it took the pharmacy quite a while to sort out the right labels on their bottles after he'd finished tinkering with them.

The job of officers mess NCO was also out of the question since a steward's inquiry' into the watering of the whiskey and gin bottles had pointed the finger firmly at poor Tommy, while the matron and the nurses were still baying for his blood after he'd taken it upon himself to supervise and dispense the treatment of some of the children in the nearby Families Wing.

The issue of his appointment now surfaced once again. Despite his colourful past history, I was loath to lose a man of his obvious talents, not least because he had a deep and committed attachment to all things medical and was also a first-class operator on active service in the field. There was no situation that left him stumped, no problem or emergency that left him without a solution, and he never ever panicked or lost his head.

The US army, faced with this very same problem, long ago cottoned on to the fact that these would-be medics, while loose cannons and a danger if allowed run unchecked, are a source of invaluable experience too good to lose and have instituted a programme designed to give men with limited educational standards a medical course which equips them to act as paramedics.

The only place I found willing to take Tommy on board was the dental department and, after a little persuasion, Tom McNally, the genial dental supremo, was reluctantly persuaded to give him a last chance. But after only a short time in his service, McNally confessed himself amazed at the man's competence and efficiency which for the first time in years allowed him to take it easier and enjoy the occasional game of golf, and little by little he delegated more and more authority to Tracy's control.

Things went swimmingly for a time, with McNally glowingly praising Tracy to the skies, until one Saturday morning when a crisis arose and Tom was recalled to do some emergency work in his surgery. The place would normally be deserted at weekends, so imagine his surprise to find quite a queue outside the surgery door, with children playing in the corridors and prams and buggy cars cluttering up the approaches outside. Pushing his way inside, he beheld a sight which took the wind completely out of his sails.

There stood Treacy in pristine white gown, drill in one hand, mouth mirror in the other, leaning over a reclining figure in the chair as he murmured solicitously "Open wide dear, this won't hurt a bit."

Now even for the placid-natured McNally this was going a bit too far, and Tracy was immediately clapped in irons and placed in close confinement for the rest of the weekend. The following Monday morning, an urgent top-level conference of all the hospital brass took place to try to resolve the Tracy problem once and for all.

Angry opinions were being freely expressed, with the majority running strongly in favour of dismissal, when Doc Cahill, who had served with Tommy overseas and appreciated his real worth, uttered the immortal lines which probably saved his bacon.

"Yes," he admitted, "Tracy's a menace and no mistake. But if there's another war, and he's dropped into the middle of the jungle, OK he'll kill hundreds - but he'll save millions!"

You'd need at least one book, maybe two, to do justice to Des Rooney. Almost every night of his life was spent at the dogs, his real true love, although he did manage to fit in the occasional horse-race meeting as well, in addition to spending a good deal of his time in the bookmaker's shops.

Of course all this activity left very little time for work and he was continually ducking and diving, trying hard not to be conspicuous but, weighing at least twenty two stone, not succeeding too well. Try as he might to hide it, everyone seemed to know what he was up to, and when Col. Tommy Fox, a shrewd little Northerner, asked Des at a conference why he hadn't complied with some direction or other he'd been given, he immediately launched into a tortuous rigmarole in the hope of confusing the issue.

He was simply too busy, he told the highly sceptical Tommy, he had so many tasks on hand - he was involved in reorganising transport duties, he was assistant mess secretary as well, and besides all that he was a member of an audit doing the accounts in the NCOs mess. Now all these, while undoubtedly necessary, were basically Mickey Mouse jobs and Tommy well knew it.

He gazed silently at Des for a few moments. "Lt. Rooney," he announced crushingly. "A good corporal could do all that."

"Ah yes, sir," sighed Des sympathetically. "But where would you get a good corporal?" Even Tommy Fox had no answer to that.

The sight of his gargantuan figure thumbing a lift soon became a familiar landmark on the roadside. One Monday morning, as the Chief of Staff was heading for the Curragh for his annual inspection of the hospital, who should he spot but the huge figure of Rooney standing at Newlands Cross, frantically trying to hitch a lift in a desperate attempt to get down before the Chief did. Of course everyone else in the car spotted him as well, but the Chief, who was fond of a gamble himself, pretended to be reading his newspaper and never let on a thing. Now that's what you call class.

Shortly after that, we decided to acquire a few dogs of our own. Naming them provided a lot of fun. One in particular, 'Camp Adjutant', rose a few hackles when Sergeant Pop Hayes mischievously informed the real camp adjutant that he'd heard it was shortly to be shot because, like it's name-sake, it was "dodgy and totally fucking useless!" Fortunately for us, the man had a sense of humour.

But despite the fact that we were now getting the best of inside information straight from the horse's mouth via the chaplain, who'd married many of the trainers and jockeys and baptised their children, we were still regularly losing our 'cobblers' at the track. Angry creditors were literally beating at our door while bankruptcy loomed just around the corner, with the very real danger of getting ourselves cashiered from the army into the bargain.

The chaplain was lucky enough to have the Sunday church collection to keep him afloat, otherwise he'd have starved to death, but for the rest of us the twelfth of every month became a regular nightmare as we desperately tried to raise the funds to pay our mess bills on time. Paying the mess bill was absolutely essential. You could set the barracks on fire, do a runner with the mess funds, you could even get the colonel's daughter in foal and you still might get away with it - but fail to pay your mess bill and it was curtains for certain.

The chit system was the problem - no cash was involved at all. You simply paid for your drinks by signing a chit for the amount and then settling the account by the twelfth of the following month. Unfortunately it was all too easy to run up a hefty bill without hardly noticing, and many officers' bar bills regularly exceeded their monthly cheques, necessitating a visit to the bank manager or a hasty trip to see the folks at home.

Des was a particularly hopeless gambling case. Even though he was a genius at readying up a dog for a 'stroke', and we did manage to pull off a number of successful coups, he was simply unable to resist punting on all the other races as well, even the photo-finishes, which was clearly a recipe for the knacker's yard.

As a result he was always under pressure, cashing cheques, redeeming post-dated ones which he'd almost forgotten about, and travelling long distances all over the country to borrow enough money from his friends to bail him out of his current scrape even heading over to Spike Island by boat where his good friend Mick O'Driscoll held sway, where he could lie low for a few days.

But no matter how low his morale during the day, he'd come to life at the greyhound track at night, like an addict who'd just had a good snort of coke. He'd then be a picture of non-stop action, taking tips from shady characters, running to the tote, talking to the tic-tac man, dodging the bookies he owed money to, doing the jackpot, cheering home winners, and shaking his head in disgust whenever he backed a loser.

The physical toll was crippling. We were on the go day and night, practically meeting ourselves coming back from one race-meeting or another, usually broke and a little tipsy, and pretty soon all the excitement and all the late nights began to take their toll. But while Des had been operating like that for years and obviously thrived on it, there was a definite limit to my stamina, both physical and financial.

My athletics career also began to suffer due to lack of training, and so a hard decision had to be made. Reluctantly, I decided to bite the bullet and cut out all racing and gambling until I got my act together again, which of course meant giving Des a wide berth. This presented him with the problem of finding transport but he soon solved that by teaming up with a soft-hearted nurse from the military hospital who just happened to drive a Mini, and it was simply hilarious to see the pair of them heading off to the races, with Des at the wheel and the Mini listing dangerously to port.

Shortly after that he was posted south on promotion. The next I heard was when the bomb squad was called to blow up his suitcase on the barrack square in Limerick, after he'd left it ticking away unattended in the bar while he foraged for grub in the kitchen. When the bomb squad had finished, all that remained was a pile of tattered old form books and the shattered remains of an alarm clock.

But while my bank balance undoubtedly took a turn for the better and my athletics career revived somewhat, I still hankered after the excitement of those heady days, the pressure, the thrills, the photo-finishes. It was perhaps only fitting that the bookmakers, never an emotional breed, stood for a minute's silence in Shelbourne Park on the night that Big Des died.

What better epitaph could a man want than that?

Twenty Three
The Mission

You can bring a horse to water, but you can't make him drink; you can march the troops to the church, but you can't make them pray. Down through the centuries, probably dating from the Crusades, a strangely ambivalent relationship has existed between religion and the military. On the one hand, stringent preparations are undertaken to cripple, maim or kill the enemy, while on the other elaborate religious ceremonies are devised to excuse or palliate the slaughter, which seems a strange contradiction in terms.

In olden days druids and assorted holymen were enlisted to call down a curse and strike dread into the opposition, while raising home morale by casting a spell which prevented them, in theory at least, from suffering death or injury at the hands of the enemy.

In more modern times chaplains were officially accredited to different units, accompanying them into battle and even jumping by parachute into enemy lines when required, indeed, the very first chaplains may well have been attached to Irish troops on the continent in battle. But whatever their history, undoubtedly some see them as a great consolation when facing death or injury, confronted with that final leap into the unknown.

Brendan Behan possibly put his finger accurately on the pulse when asked what religion he professed. "I'm a daylight atheist," he replied, a pragmatic opinion with which many would identify, and indeed there are very few who'd refuse any such consolation as may be available to them in the lonely frightening hours prior to going into battle. In our own army, religious ceremonies are part and parcel of military celebrations, reflecting the deep personal faith of many men. The most striking of these is the sword salute delivered by the officer guard of honour during the consecration of the mass, which is always accompanied by a trumpet salute.

It was customary for every barracks in the Curragh to hold a mass parade every Sunday and holy day which everyone living in barracks was obliged to attend, though this often caused a good deal of grumbling and resentment. To make matters worse, the head chaplain then decided to beef things up further by holding an additional parade on the first Thursday of every month, to coincide with the tradition of the First Friday.

The troops responded to this by either disappearing undetected from the church or, if that proved impossible, by defiantly falling asleep and snoring their heads off as soon as they got settled in their seats, the only interruption being the chaplain's droning sermon threatening dire consequences if they failed to repent.

He had obviously failed to spot what everyone else knew - you can perhaps cow civilian audiences, but you can't browbeat battle-hardened troops and get away with it. How anyone could expect to intimidate men who had many times faced death or injury, often in a hostile environment far from home, beats me.

About the only time I ever remember the troops paying any attention was when a Belgian army chaplain, Fr. Rougeau, arrived in the Curragh for an extended stay. Mounting the pulpit one Thursday afternoon, he electrified the men by telling them of his own experiences as a machine gunner in the trenches during World War One. Those still asleep were rudely nudged awake by their companions lest they miss a word of his dramatic sermon, something they could at last appreciate and identify with.

He told of first-hand experience of life in the trenches; of massed bayonet charges, of exploding shells ripping bodies to pieces; of gas attacks, hunger, cold and exhaustion; of rats eating the frozen corpses before they could be buried; of the feelings of loneliness, rage, sorrow and terror, all those inexplicable personal emotions peculiar to fighting men in armies everywhere.

They sat there in their seats, entranced, as he painted a grim picture of four years of hell in the bloody mud of Flanders, that hopeless aimless struggle which wiped away the flower of Europe's youth in a macabre dance of death, but which also planted the personal seed of faith which had led him to talk to them that very afternoon.

You could hear a pin drop as he spoke. They hung on his every word, spoken in heavily-accented English, visibly moved, and they didn't want him to finish, and when afterwards he came outside to meet the men, they crowded around as if he were the new Messiah, anxious to shake his hand and welcome him to the camp.

Sadly, Fr. Rougeau didn't tarry long - within a year he was dead from cancer. He was buried in the local cemetery with full military honours, amid a huge attendance of off-duty soldiers who had identified with him in such a poignant fashion, signifying the deep respect that one soldier has for another old soldier who has looked into the jaws of death and lived to tell the tale.

As with most parishes in Ireland, the annual church mission took place during Lent and usually lasted a couple of weeks, culminating in a full-dress parade to church on the final day, complete with pipe and brass bands and officer guard of honour. Missionary priests from outside were usually employed to whip the troops into line, since a change from their own familiar chaplains was deemed advisable. The previous year, the mission had been deemed a bit of a flop because the missionaries, accustomed to more docile congregations, had been far too polite and a little in awe of the troops, appealing to their better natures and relying on exhortations to work the oracle. That approach was guaranteed to fail.

This time things were different. In came the heavy gang, in the form of Fathers Joe Drumgoole and Jack Whelan, two veteran warriors of the tough no-nonsense parishes of Dublin's inner-city Arran Quay where they'd eat you alive without salt.

The two of them could drink, swear, punt and play cards with the best, and every day they'd visit a different barracks listening to the men and what they had to say, hearing their confessions, and blessing them, their families and their homes.

But in the evenings things changed altogether. Now was the time for the chaplains to take them on again on their home ground - in the canteens, in the mess bars, in the poker schools, whatever battleground they chose. And they'd stay as long as the action lasted, swapping yarns and singing songs until finally the approach of dawn signalled it was time to hit the hay, but then at early morning mass the pair would be back in action again, exhorting, singing hymns, pounding the pulpit. It was great stuff, and the men loved it.

A feature of the Drummer's mass would be when he'd laughingly welcome some bleary-eyed late-comer from the altar steps with the greeting - "Ah, sure it's yourself, Pat. Decent of you to come." At this the red-faced man, who'd only recently been drinking with the pair of them in some bar or other, would slink shamefacedly into the nearest pew, to the delighted grins of his pals.

Judging by the attendances at mass and the sacraments, their mission was a roaring success. I don't know if the two priests took a holiday or not after it was all over but, if they didn't they deserved to. It was incredible how they managed to last the pace for those two whole weeks but far from collapsing, they actually seemed to thrive on it.

Sadly, we didn't ever get to see the pair of them again, because word of their success got around and they were booked up solidly every year after that. But no one will easily forget the valiant efforts they made - tough, hardy men of the world like them understood what really made soldiers tick, but even more importantly, what turned them off. Instead of supplications and pious appeals, they gave 'em hell, fire and brimstone and duly reaped the rewards.

*

The tricky problem of obtaining parity of pay and gratuities for single men in the army had defied a solution down over the years, but now I felt it was time for my generation to take on the challenge. The more I looked at it, the more I couldn't understand how such a blatant injustice had been condoned for so long.

Even now, when people rightfully express amazement as to how the army ever allowed such a system to operate or how single men tolerated it, they fail to understand that for anyone to dare challenge the system back then was considered almost mutinous. If you took on the system, and especially if you won, you were a marked man.

Pay for both married and single officers had always been the same right up until 1938, but then some clever dick of a civil servant introduced a married fuel and light allowance into the pay structure as a device for gaining further income. Though this allowance was initially minute, before you could say Cock Robin a breach suddenly existed between married and single basic pay which naturally enough widened with every subsequent percentage pay increase.

Within a period of ten to fifteen years, a single man was being paid about half that of his married counterpart, all for doing the same job. And by the time he'd paid income tax, his pay was even less than half, a situation which by any stretch of the imagination couldn't be justified, though the authorities did try.

But even worse than that, single men were denied any gratuity on leaving the army, in contrast to their married counterparts who benefited generously. Since a gratuity is a bounty for services rendered, the denial of this facility for performing precisely the same job was nothing short of scandalous. A married officer could qualify for a tax-free gratuity of anything between £15,000 and £25,000 on retirement during the 60's and 70's, depending on rank and time served, but a single officer didn't even get a sausage.

With a view to rectifying this situation, I organised a meeting of all the single officers in the camp and included in the list four colourful senior captains who were shortly to retire sans gratuity. Des Rooney, gambler extraordinaire, headed the list, Joe Bowles came next, while Joe Higgins and Denis Mellerick brought up the rear. We assembled one Friday night in the snug bar in McDermott officers mess to plan future strategy, full of hope and confidence, but then occurred one of the most bizarre meetings it has ever been my misfortune to attend.

I opened the meeting by outlining the problem and set out the progress which had been made in the campaign so far, pointing out that bar-stool waffle achieved nothing, from now on every action had to be coordinated and calculated. Verbal complaints, I stressed, were worse than useless and didn't even merit a reply, every submission had to made be in writing in order to build a reference file in the department of defence. Then Martin Cafferty, afterwards a noted legal beak, set out his vision of how best to tackle the problem and made a series of proposals on the best way forward.

For a moment there was silence, then all hell broke loose. First Des Rooney leapt angrily to his feet, brandishing a race-card from Harold's Cross greyhound track on which was scrawled the personal telephone number of Jerry Cronin, the minister for defence, himself another keen doggie-man.

"I met the minister at the dogs last night," Des told the meeting excitedly. "And I gave him two winners, one at 5/2 and the other at three to one, and he bought me a drink in the bar and I told him all about the problem and he wrote it down on the back of his race-card and he promised me faithfully he'd do something about it." Complete silence greeted this sally.

Next Joe Bowles took the floor. A scratch golfer from Clonmel, Joe was a stalwart forward with Bective Rangers RFC for a number of years and an outstanding swimmer as well, in fact I remembered watching as a boy while he swept all before him at an army gala held in my own home-town in Waterford. He also had this confusing habit of referring to people as 'your man' or 'your other man' which usually had no bearing whatever on the matter in hand.

"I told your man about it the last time we met," began Joe.

"And he promised he'd have a word with your other man about it, but I haven't heard a word since. Maybe I should have another word with your man again." At the end, we were none the wiser and his unlikely proposal was also greeted with silence.

Joe Higgins from artillery then took the stage. Widely read, Joe took an avid interest in political affairs, especially civil war politics, and told the meeting in his lilting West Cork accent about the verbal representations he'd made to various politicians over the years and how they hadn't even had the good manners to reply.

"Oh Chrissshht, the bastards, the perfidious bastards," Joe growled, rubbing his close-cropped hair in a paroxysm of rage. "I've lost all faith in politicians, they're all the bloody same. And as for this present crowd, they're nothing but a shower of Blueshirts." Another long silence.

Last up was Denis Mellerick, the artistic leader of the No. 3 Army Band, who'd briefly served a tenure in a seminary as a youth and still retained contacts in high ecclesiastical circles. "It's a bloody disgrace," he pouted, lower lip protruding petulantly. "I told the monsignor about it the last time we met but nothing happened. But maybe I should go higher. Yes, that's it, I'll get on to the bishop, we were in the seminary together" And with that he sat down, head nodding in satisfaction, looking all around him for approval. Silence also greeted this effort.

Within minutes, the four of them stood grouped around the bar counter shouting at one another at the tops of their voices, swilling pints and half-whiskies to beat the band and arguing away vociferously about the pet complaints that had exercised their minds for years, all to no avail. All semblance of order or any ideas for formulating future policy had now disappeared and, as they bellowed and shouted, I could only stare in astonishment, disheartened by this display. Just then I felt a tap on my shoulder - it was Martin Cafferty, a look of disgust on his face.

"Come on away out of here before we go mad as well," he growled, and off we marched through the hall portals and out into the night. Not one of the four even noticed we were going, so engrossed were they in their arguments, but if that night's shenanigans were anything to go by it was transparently obvious why the gratuity problem had persevered all those years. And as we walked away, the loud echo of their voices preceded us down along the long marble corridors.

It was clear that a new approach to the problem needed to be adopted, one which didn't rely too heavily on older men like the Four Horsemen in the bar who, while willing, really believed in their heart of hearts that they couldn't win, could never beat the system. And if anyone in these more enlightened days asks why single people hadn't tried harder, hadn't fought tooth and nail to change this anomaly, perhaps the story of Col. 'Slim' Donoghue tells it all.

Slim was the OC Military College who, in a fit of pique at having to pay for his accommodation, decided to make a stand. As a married man living away from home, he felt this levy was unjustified and, to prove his point, sensationally decided to pitch a tent on the front lawn of the officers mess in Pearse Barracks, in full view of everyone, and move in with all his goods and chattels. He then took on the system headlong by refusing point blank to pay for his room in the mess which, as he pointed out, was now obviously unoccupied.

I need hardly tell you that this dramatic gesture caused quite a stir in higher army echelons, as well as exciting the enthusiasm of every single officer in the army who felt that at long last they had found someone with the spunk to fight their cause. But sadly, nemesis was close at hand.

Shortly afterwards a direct fire-order arrived, signed by the Chief of Staff and addressed to Slim, reclining in his opulent tented palace - vacate the lawn and re-occupy your room immediately, or else face the consequences. No doubting the seriousness of this situation.

The outcome was predictable, if disappointing. Slim lost the argument, and his pride too, when he meekly folded his tent and crept back inside the mess, tail between his legs, and not another peep was ever heard about the injustice of having to pay for unoccupied accommodation or about unequal pay and gratuities for single men from that day onwards. If Slim Donoghue couldn't do it, the reasoning went, who could?

But there was a lesson to be learnt from all this, which is that one should never provoke an argument unless one is sure of winning. With Martin Cafferty's help, a systematic study of army regulations soon revealed a loophole. Because the excuse put forward by the authorities was that married officers needed rehabilitation on leaving the army, whereas single officers didn't, I now decided to challenge the system head-on by leaving my barracks accommodation and taking up residence in an apartment in nearby Newbridge.

This was a deliberate ploy to challenge the idea that only married men needed to be rehoused, the very reason advanced by the authorities for refusing to give single men a gratuity. But in fact it was glaringly obvious that single men needed rehabilitating every bit as much if not more because they had nowhere to go on leaving the army and had no gratuity either to enable them to purchase accommodation, whereas the vast majority of married men owned their own house.

It was also not without significance that every statistic published by agencies for the homeless or organisations like the Simon Community pointed up the fact that many of their clients are ex-army and mostly single.

As expected, my action had the desired effect. Within days I found myself served with disciplinary charges, no less than three in all, the primary one of which was 'failing to obey a lawful order', a very serious charge indeed for an officer. I was arraigned before the GOC Curragh, a preliminary hearing held to decide whether or not there were sufficient grounds for sending me forward for court martial.

But when your back is right to the wall, your brain often functions more sharply. After rummaging for days through army regulations, I discovered a fatal flaw in their armament, an obscure clause in the regulations which allowed me to live out of barracks without permission, provided that I was willing to pay for the accommodation provided.

Of course I was willing to pay, I told the court, although I also gave notice that I intended to challenge that aspect just as soon as this present matter was out of the way. Despite the opposition's objections, all charges were immediately dismissed, leaving me the victor on the day.

But that was only the thin edge of the wedge. Flushed with this success, I now decided to mount a challenge against the right of the department of defence to charge me rent for unused accommodation, the very argument on which Slim Donoghue had foundered all those years previously. And I was feeling pretty confident of success - I had them on the run, and had every intention on putting the boot in without mercy.

Within a short week, my application had been granted and I was free to live where I liked, when I liked. Now the time had come to tackle the issue of equal pay and gratuities head-on, but there was to be no easy path. Every letter had to be meticulously answered, every prevarication challenged, every contention contested, but gradually, bit by bit, communique by slow communique, we built up a bulging file in the Department of Defence where previously none had existed. Now every query had to be treated with respect by the authorities where previously it had been allowed to gather dust in a file somewhere and ignored.

Fighting this battle was an experience I wouldn't have missed for the world. Besides the obvious injustice of the thing, it was fascinating to pit one's brains against a seemingly immovable immutable force, an unseeing, uncaring establishment, and try to outwit it. You had to figure out how these things worked, to find out how the various departments operated, and try to reach the ear of those with the real power.

It also provided a startling insight into the perversity of human beings. To watch people with no personal stake at all in the affair go out of their way to throw a spanner in the works, just out of sheer 'pig-iron', was an education in itself, but whatever the reason, they came crawling out of the woodwork one after the other in a seemingly endless stream.

My own CO was the worst offender of all. A recent impor-
tation from the Army Equitation School, more accustomed to
handling dumb animals than fractious officers, he refused
point-blank to allow my letters to go forward on the grounds
that I was in danger of rocking his boat and somehow damaging his promotion prospects, and I had to threaten to send the
letters directly over his head to the minister, as was my right,
before he finally cracked.

One might just as easily wonder at the lack of 'cojones' of
those single officers who stood to benefit most and should
have done something, but for whatever reason - native cun-
ning, fear of authority, cowardice or whatever - sat on the
fence and never lifted a finger.

Having won one battle, the rest now became easier. One by
one, point by laborious point, our team picked off the opposition's arguments. And once it became obvious that the opposition had failed to crush us and we were still standing, valuable
inside information began to arrive from various sources, from
orderly room sergeants, from unit adjutants, even from civil
servants, intelligence which enabled us to pre-empt the opposition's next move and strike home first.

Finally, just as we were about to challenge the matter in the
courts, an EEC directive settled the matter in our favour once
and for all. At long last justice had won through, even though
it was by now too late for many decent people who'd left the
army with no gratuity at all to show for their efforts. I didn't
benefit much myself, sad to say, due to service restrictions, but
at least it was nice to taste victory for a change, and I would-
n't be truthful if I didn't admit to a certain satisfaction at giving the opposition a bloody nose.

But no victory is won without a price. My overseas
prospects virtually disappeared, marked as I had now
become with the tag of 'difficult', 'individualistic' and 'awkward', or similar convenient labels to justify non-selection.
No point in in being bitter about that side of things. I took the
decision to fight knowing full well that there would be a price
to pay but this was one fight I badly wanted to win, not just

for myself, but for all those NCOs and men who depended on me and people like me to do something. But give a dog a bad name .....

Twenty Four
A Dog's Life

But besides the pressures I had to endure in the barracks, I was also under severe pressure from other quarters, especially the banks, because of the high life I was leading. Like Des Rooney, who boasted of no less than fifteen separate accounts in various parts of the country which he juggled constantly, I'd now acquired two accounts in Newbridge, one with the Bank of Ireland in the main street and the other a short distance away with AIB.

As it happened, the two bank managers were decent enough fellows with whom I often shared a social drink, but they had a job to do and couldn't allow people like me to carouse, drink, and gamble to our hearts content without at some stage calling us to account. I'd regularly receive phone calls and missives to come and see them to discuss the state of my finances, but of course completely ignored them all and continued on my merry way without a care for the future. The calls became ever more insistent and threatening.

Finally, under dire threat of being reported to my superiors, I agreed to go see Gerry O'Mahoney of AIB in his spanking new offices in Newbridge. Now this wasn't as big a threat as Gerry thought because most of my superiors were themselves under pressure from banks and had no sympathy whatever for bankers. Gerry, a chain-smoker, fogged fag after fag as he sat there sifting through the mass of papers littering his desk in an effort to isolate my accounts, while I sat across from him patiently waiting.

"Now, Michael, and what plans do you have to reduce your outstanding commitments?" he enquired, frowning at me over his bi-focal glasses. "You haven't us paid a cent in months."

186

Of course I hadn't any plans whatsoever but knew that was-n't what he wanted to hear, so I started waffling away trying to spin some yarn about all the ways I had in mind to reduce costs and make some money. Gerry interrupted me impatiently.

"Yes yes, I know all that, but have you any collateral?"

I scarcely knew the meaning of the word, but decided to try and reassure him that I was indeed a man of means. "Well, I do have some bloodstock," I began, somewhat hesitantly. At this his face brightened.

"Ah, bloodstock," he purred, thinking no doubt of brood-mares with foals at foot. "And what bloodstock have you got? Mares, foals, colts, whatever?"

"Well no," I replied innocently. "I haven't actually got any mares or foals" - his face fell - "but I do have eighteen grey-hounds." At this he completely lost the rag.

"Greyhounds! Greyhounds!" he roared. "You call that bloodstock? Get the hell out of here and don't be wasting my time." And with that he rang the bell and had me ushered unceremoniously out of his office, his final imprecation ring-ing in my ears. "You'll be hearing from me."

I'd fully intended doing the double act and taking in a visit to the Bank of Ireland after the AIB, but after that razzing from Gerry I was too shaken to face another grilling, so I got some-one to ring Donal Shannon and inform him that I wasn't avail-able right now because I'd been sent to Salisbury in England on an explosives course and wouldn't be back for some weeks.

I deliberately included the word 'explosives' in the fond hope of making those in the bank realise just how dangerous my work really was and how they should perhaps show me more respect, but alas, they couldn't have cared less. I was to go see the manager as a matter of urgency, the caller was told, the moment I returned from England.

As it happened, the very next day I was due to go hunting with Naas Harriers, the local pack of hounds which hunted the area all around Kilcullen, Kildare and Athy. I'd be safe there, I reckoned, because the pack never came anywhere near

Newbridge and so there was little danger of my cover being blown.

It was a great day's hunting in that brilliant jumping country around Kilcullen stretching towards Carnalway Cross, Calverstown and Bolton Hill. I was mounted on a magnificent beast, a 12 year-old ex-Equitation School gelding which had won Grand Prix events in Rome and Zurich, and he gave me the thrill of a lifetime, there wasn't a fence or hedge that he didn't fearlessly take in his stride. Gerry Enright and Roy Bennett were also well-mounted with me on the hunt because it was army policy to keep these former top jumpers in the Curragh for use by cadets and officers rather than have them put down, and the staff were only too happy to have competent riders exercise them.

It was a bright, brisk winter's day and the fox was in high fettle, and the hunt went helter-skelter across rolling country almost without a break, chased by the pack of yelping hounds led by their intrepid huntsmaster, former champion jockey Paddy Powell.

As these things go, the light faded fast late in the afternoon and finally the fox swung around in a grand circle and finished up almost exactly back where he began, in the territory with which he was most familiar. Here Paddy called a halt, and the handful of us who were still in touch were left stranded in the area around Great Connell on the Naas side of Newbridge.

This left us with no option but to take the shortest route home, and so our troupe set off for home, posting wearily through the main street of Newbridge. But then to my horror, just as I passed the Bank of Ireland, there was the manager himself, Donal Shannon, coming out of the front door. Attracted by the clattering of the hooves, he turned around to watch the horses passing and instantly spotted my mud-splattered figure perched up on the back of my nag, merrily posting my way back to the stables.

He stopped and stared, standing stock-still on the steps with his hands on his hips, adjusting his rimless glasses to get a better look at the spectacle. Some of the by-standers waved and cheered and, not to be outdone, I gallantly lifted my bowler hat in salutation as I passed, which was the very least I could do under the circumstances.

This gave Donal such a shock he had to retire to Coffeys pub afterwards to recover. Bank managers like to meet one another after hours in bar snugs, to talk shop and discuss the day's trading and ruminate over financial transactions and shifting world money patterns.

"By the Lord Jaysus, Gerry," Donal told the bemused O'Mahoney. "You'll never guess what I saw today."

He immediately launched into a diatribe about the return of the hunters and their horses, bemoaning the fact that some people were able to enjoy a great day's hunting while the pair of them had to work. In O'Mahoney he found a sympathetic ear. "Donal, " he announced soberly, sipping his whiskey gingerly. "They're getting away with murder. Where did we go wrong?"

Of course the next day the phones to the Curragh hopped and I was summoned to Newbridge to account for my misdoings, but following the expected ritual going-over, Donal then invited me to join Gerry and himself in Coffey's pub to celebrate our new arrangements, which was all very civilised indeed. Whatever else might be said about them, and that was plenty, it can't be said they lacked a sense of humour.

All this time my stable of greyhounds kept growing and growing. I now had eighteen dogs of all shapes, sexes and sizes which I raced at the various tracks around the area - Mullingar, Navan, Newbridge - and occasionally, if they were good enough, at the two Dublin tracks, Harold's Cross and Shelbourne Park.

Looking after them was quite a chore and very time-consuming, but I was lucky in that the main donkey work of cleaning kennels, feeding and walking was done by orderly Pte. Mick Carey, who'd worked as a professional dog handler during his time in England. Mick was on the easy list due to asthma, so it provided him with a welcome bit of exercise to take the dogs walking every day. I returned from leave one day to find Mick in a state of panic. "Sir, the dogs are gone," he wheezed. "And they're going to be shot tomorrow."

"And who's going to shoot 'em," I enquired, smiling at his apparent joke. But I soon discovered it was no joke, the dogs had indeed gone, impounded by the military police on the orders of the Provost Marshal whose responsibility it was. On further inquiring, I was told with no little amount of glee that I should take a look at daily routine orders, where the notice of the impounding and pending execution had been posted during my absence.

Further enquiries revealed that there was now nothing that could be done, the dogs were to be disposed of the following day. The Provost Marshal, who harboured a grudge, took pleasure in informing me that it was now too late to do anything, the matter had already been decided.

That was like a red rag to a bull. It was bad enough impounding my dogs without my permission, but to do so while I was on leave was a gutless and sneaky action which just couldn't be let away without challenge.

I got on the phone post-haste to Jim Byrne, chairman of Wicklow GAA, who lived in Baltinglass. At the time I was training both the Baltinglass and Wicklow football teams and we had become firm friends. Jim was a fearless descendant of the great 1798 hero Michael O'Dwyer and a veteran of the modern-day Battle of Baltinglass, but far more importantly, he was also a part-owner of one of the dogs, as was Godfrey Timmins, the Chief Whip of the Fine Gael party. As soon as he heard the news, Jim rang Leinster House and before the afternoon was out, Godfrey and himself were poised at HQ in Ceannt Barracks, demanding to see the GOC.

As luck would have it, the GOC Tom McDonald was related to Jim by marriage, and as soon as he heard their story and had it confirmed by me in person, the telephone wires were humming angrily to the Provost Marshal's office and to the camp dog pound. Within an hour or so the dogs were on their way back to their kennels in McDermott barracks, and those who a short time previously had taken delight in putting me under pressure now had to eat humble pie and publicly apologise for their hasty actions.

To make them grovel even further, I insisted on them kenneling the dogs in person and kept them there while I carried out an inspection, which was sweet revenge.

For years I'd managed to stall undergoing a Command & Staff course, but finally in 1972 was finally forced to capitulate as gracefully as possible. I reported to the Military College, armed with oodles of manuscripts and precis, acres of rules and regulations and, of course, bundles of maps wrapped tightly in cellophane, putting me in mind of the old Emergency refrain - "

"Hi ho, hi ho,
  As off to war we go,
  With maps and charts,
  And porter farts,
  Hi ho, hi ho."

My reason for previously refusing to undergo this course was because it was conducted through the medium of Irish which, quite frankly, was absolutely ludicrous and just another example of political correctness gone crazy. Far from being anti-Irish, in fact I'm from an Irish-speaking area and have a deep respect and affection for the language and culture, but I considered this was both demeaning to the language and the quality of the course which had always been first-class.

Every evening students were issued with mountains of precis written in both Irish and English on an amazing variety of subjects, from man-management techniques to global strategy, to brigade/division structures, to psychological operations (psy/ops), to modern developments in weaponry, all which you were expected to study overnight and be prepared to debate in class next morning, but most of the time was lost in translating thoughts from English back into Irish and vice-versa.

As a result the one-on-one debates, such a valuable feature of the C&S course, were greatly hampered by the lack of fluency and competence in the language of both the instructors and the students, many of whom had only the barest knowledge of Irish.

It was sometimes painful to listen to them attempting to debate an important issue, such as psy/ops or the techniques of deploying troops to combat urban guerrilla warfare, by employing a collection of stock phrases and cliches to try to fill the gaps.

The C&S course, of nine months duration, is pretty intensive and arduous, involving a lot of study and being continually academically challenged by the dedicated instructors, but one incident helped lighten the burden. The OC Military College, Ferdy Lee, a lovely old gent of the old school with silvery hair and a bristling moustache, was at the lectern busily thanking the German dare-devil pilot who'd just delivered a lecture on his wartime exploits to the course.

"Col. Skorzeny, on behalf of the 42nd C&S Course, allow me to thank you," said Ferdy in fluent German, clicking his heels and bowing towards the distinguished visitor.

"Ah, dankishen, Colonel," replied Skorzeny, also clicking his heels and bowing. Not to be outdone, Ferdy bowed and clicked his heels again, to which Skorzeny replied in similar fashion, and the pair of them went on like this for several more moments like a pair of praying Mantis, before the bemused students started to applaud and finally broke the spell.

To make matters worse, snow started to fall heavily as the they filed out onto the barrack square towards the helicopter, accompanied by the Chief-of-Staff and his aide-de camp, with all the students lining the windows to watch their departure. As the chopper revved noisily in preparation for take-off, the blades set up a veritable blizzard of white snow-flakes which completely enveloped Ferdie who was standing rigidly to attention saluting, looking for all the world like a tousled Santa Claus.

The chopper circled as it rose slowly into the air and as it did so, Ferdy also circled with it, standing there in a daze looking upwards and still saluting long after it had disappeared from view. Only the cheering and thumping of window-panes by us disrespectful students woke him from his reverie.

The pressure I was under now began to ease off, almost certainly as a result of these latest victories over unfeeling authority. People who'd previously looked askance, even if they didn't quite try to put the boot in, now began to act in a more friendly fashion, even asking me to join them in a drink if we met in the bar and things like that.

My reputation had obviously preceded me, because while there were those who mightn't exactly like my style, nonetheless they began to treat me with a new respect. Even the brass began to act in a more friendly fashion, going out of their way to show that they held no grudges, it was best to let sleeping dogs lie.

I now seemed to be regarded as a figure of some stature, one who'd somehow earned his spurs and who deserved to be treated with amused affection. The sight of myself surrounded at the bar in the clubhouse after the all-army hurling final, being bought drinks by a Chief of Staff and three serving generals raised many an eyebrow, but of course that was no more than it should be. No point in holding grudges, no sense in prolonging enmities over past events which after all are ultimately unimportant in the end.

But with most of the things I'd wanted to now achieved, and with no honourable cause to fight, I felt it was time to look further afield. The army had taught me many new skills, not least the ability to survive under pressure, but also those of leadership, marksmanship, toughness of body and spirit, knowledge of weapons and explosives, and physical expertise, but now the time had come to seek pastures new.

My farewell party in the officers mess is still talked about, and I must admit to being touched by the good wishes of the many NCOs and men, particularly the single ones, which happily I retain to this day. That alone made it all worthwhile. A number of my friends tried to talk me out of leaving, pointing out, possibly tongue in cheek, the bright career that could still lie ahead if only I agreed to conform and play ball.

To this I tried to explain, as patiently as I could, that my biggest problem, and the real reason for my leaving, was boredom, I'd simply got fed up with my cushy administrative job in the military hospital which even a semi-trained orang-utan could have done without too much bother.

At this Roger McCorley, who'd been waiting his chance for years, perked up and went straight for the jugular. "Mick", he smirked, "perhaps he was!", leaving me for once completely stumped. We all need friends like that to keep our egos in check.

Epilogue

It is never easy to admit that you have been wrong; it is harder still to admit to having harboured inbuilt prejudices for the past thirty eight years. Ever since the Battle of Jadotville in July 1961, I firmly subscribed to the belief, widespread throughout the army, that C Company, the defending garrison in Jadotville, had failed to fight on, had chucked in the towel, had shown the white feather; by surrendering his position, the company commander, Comdt. Pat Quinlan, had recklessly exposed his men to the most appalling danger by submitting them to the tender mercies of ill-disciplined black troops hell-bent on vengeance. I lived with that belief all those years, confident that the continuing silence of the defenders merely confirmed that it was all true.

It was only when I began to write an account of the Battle of Jadotville and began to interview some of the survivors in depth that the full extent of the injustice perpetrated began to strike home. For the very first time I heard an entirely new version of events, a bitter, dignified, impassioned account which cast doubts on the official version which had been accepted as gospel truth all those years.

And the army encouraged me in my prejudices. By their very failure to hold an enquiry into the events at Jadotville and Lufira, by failing to fully investigate and take sworn statements from all the people involved, those in authority in the army showed a craven cowardice which unjustifiably exposed the survivors of Jadotville to the ongoing ridicule, nay, contempt, of their comrades in arms.

Many of the survivors of Jadotville whom I interviewed I personally know to be brave and honourable men. In no case did I ever feel that I was being manipulated, never once was I

195

conscious of any attempt to put a new slant on events in the hope of being rehabilitated, of somehow being allowed to wriggle off the hook.

I therefore decided to pen a new and more detailed account of the Battle of Jadotville based on my reading of the official and unofficial histories and on the first-hand accounts of many of the participants. I trust that the obvious limitations placed on my account by the march of time and the absence of some of the participants' views will be understood and appreciated.

It is my earnest hope that at long last the truth will finally out, that a full enquiry will be instituted which will now, even at this late stage, allow those remaining survivors to put their own version of events. I hope and trust that those presently in a position of power and responsibility in the army will at long last grasp the nettle and do the right thing. That is the very least that is owed to those brave few survivors of Jadotville.

Chapter 1.A
Disaster at Jadotville

Jadotville is a typical sprawling mining town about the size of Mullingar, situated approximately 70 miles from Elizabethville, the capital of Katanga, where the 35th Irish Battalion was stationed. The Lufira Bridge spans the river from which it takes its name, a thirty-foot wide, swift-flowing tributary of the massive Congo river with steep plunging banks of soft sandy soil.

C Company, under its commander, Comdt. Pat Quinlan, had been heavily involved in Operation Rumpunch just a couple of weeks previously. During that operation, in a lightning dawn attack, they smashed through the gates of gendarmerie HQ and captured all the mercenaries and a huge cache of arms and ammunition in double quick time, thereby rendering the gendarmerie helpless. Unfortunately for them the UN in its wisdom then decided to release their captives and booty, with subsequent disastrous results.

On arrival in Jadotville, to their astonishment they found themselves exposed to open hostility from the white inhabitants whom they were supposed to be protecting and were soon surrounded by hundreds of heavily-armed Katangese Army troops obviously intent on trouble. Their Belgian advisers, resolve stiffened by a heavy contingent of foreign mercenaries, called on the Irish to surrender.

This offer was refused. Under threat from all sides, the Irish fell back and hastily organised themselves into a defensive position at the edge of Jadotville but soon found themselves outflanked by a large force of attackers. Supplied and encouraged by the powerful Union Miniere, with its vast Belgian, French, and British financial interests, the aim of these

197

attackers was to overpower and capture C Company and use them as hostages to blackmail the UN into abandoning its policy of ending the secession of mineral-rich Katanga and uniting the Congo.

Over the next five days, the men of C Company were under continuous attack and were soon running short of food, ammunition and, most crucial of all, water. Every night the crackle of the radio brought graphic, if biased, accounts of the fighting on the BBC World Service.

According to the radio reports Irish casualties were high, with upwards of fifty men dead or wounded. Several rescue attempts had failed, the BBC reported, including one at Lufira Bridge, while plans to air-drop water supplies had also been abandoned. Repeatedly bombed and strafed by Fouga jet-fighters, their position was deemed hopeless.

The failure of a relief convoy from 31 Battalion to cross Lufira Bridge and get through to Jadotville was crucial. The progress of the rescue force, supported by a section of Swedish APCs and by a platoon of the fearsome Ghurkas, was also followed with rapt attention on the radio by the defenders in Jadotville, their hopes buoyed by expectations of deliverance, but when this rescue attempt failed to get through it must have been obvious to them that they were in a very sticky position indeed.

Back home, everyone listened enthralled to the unfolding far-away drama. Could the Jadotville garrison hold out a while longer, could they stave off disaster till the battalion could fight their way to their rescue? Surely the UN, the mighty UN, wouldn't, couldn't allow this deliberate challenge to their authority to succeed? Besides, a possible massacre of the beleaguered Irish would bring down terrible recriminations on the heads of the UN mission.

But then came the sickening news that the garrison had capitulated, surrendered, and had been ignominiously herded into a compound outside Jadotville with the face-saving compromise that they would be allowed to retain their arms.

However, this compromise was not honoured and soon

afterwards their arms and equipment were forcibly removed. Effectively they were now prisoners. An outlying platoon from the Bloods had also been surrounded but, since the main body of troops had already surrendered, they were soon persuaded that it was in their best interests to surrender as well.

Eventually the prisoners were all released and then repatriated. On their arrival back home in Athlone, a torch-light procession greeted the survivors as they marched through the town. Local dignatories hastened to add their congratulations while swarms of sobbing women and children crowded round to heap grateful thanks upon Comdt. Pat Quinlan, the heroic deliverer of their husbands, sons and brothers.

The authorities put as brave a face as possible upon the whole affair, reports were duly submitted and carefully filed away, and after a few desultory appearances and lectures the matter was gratefully laid to rest with as much dignity as possible, hopefully destined to soon gently fade away into the merciful mists of time. But while the pressure of other, newer events gradually pushed Jadotville farther and farther into the background, it persistently refused to go away, continuing to surface now and again with disturbing effects.

About a year later, at a party held in the camp gymnasium to say farewell to a departing unit and welcome home a returning one, a brutal bloody brawl erupted involving troops from the Curragh and the Western Command, in which serious injury was only avoided by stern action on the part of the PA's (Poilini Airm i.e Military Police). Boots, fists, belt buckles and bottles were freely used in a vicious free-for-all which left bleeding and broken bodies lying all over the place. Many of the injuries were so serious that some of the men had to be hospitalised.

The flare-up came when some of the Curragh men, their better feelings dimmed by alcohol, taunted the Westerners about the surrender at Jadotville, accusing them of cowardice and refusing to fight. Not surprisingly the Westerners, their pride stung to the quick by these unjustified criticisms, fought back and gave as good as they got. The violence of the passions aroused led to such gatherings being discontinued.

Rumours continued to surface from time to time, uncomfortable, nasty rumours which suggested that, far from being forced to surrender honourably in the face of overwhelming odds and increasing casualties, the Jadotville garrison had in fact shown the white feather, had chucked in the towel without fighting to the bitter end.

They hadn't shown sufficient determination, it was whispered, they could quite easily have broken out if only they had shown more guts. They were, after all, opposed by a mere gaggle of badly-trained black troops, indisciplined and ill-equipped, who had never shown any real stomach for a battle; only the threat of being shot by their white officers had forced them to attack at all.

Why, the story went, the Congolese didn't even know how to arm their mortar shells properly, otherwise dozens of Irish must have been blown to bits by all those shells dropping in on top of the defenceless troops. And as for the enemy being numerically too strong, having far superior fire-power - why, the handful of Irish casualties disproved that theory. If the battle was so fierce, if they had struggled as hard as they said, where were the casualties to prove it?

Was it true, as was rumoured, that the decision to surrender had been taken as the result of a Round Robin in which everyone had an equal say in the decision, one which many consider is just another method of passing the poisoned chalice, reflecting no credit on the commander of the defending garrison?

And what of Lufira Bridge - what of the allegation that the aborted rescue attempts had been a complete disaster due to incompetence and a lack of determination? Was it true that the rescue force might well have got across the bridge but, faced with unexpected resistance, had instead turned their backs and abandoned their comrades to their fate?

What truth, if any, lay in the rumour that Comdt. Mark Carroll, the commander of the supporting cavalry, had dismounted from his armoured car on the bridge and threatened to shoot his own leader for not showing sufficient determination to cross?

Was it also true that the commander of the supporting Indian company, in total disgust, told the Irish commanders to just 'fuck off' and leave the Indian troops to finish the job since they seemed unable or unwilling to do it themselves? Was he disciplined for his failure on his return to India?

Even more baffling than these questions was the reaction of the Army's top brass. Showing a complete lack of spunk which has been a distinguishing feature of many of them over the years, they failed to clear the air, failed to order a full enquiry into arguably the single most traumatic event in the entire history of the army.

It scarcely seems conceivable that a formal Court of Enquiry was not held at which sworn statements were taken from all the principal participants involved which would then be analysed and acted upon. This was the very least that should have been done, the very least that the participants were entitled to in order to re-establish their reputations or otherwise.

Instead, a policy of forgetfulness was adopted. Formal reports were cursorily studied, shelved, and then switched onto the back-burner. While this attitude is peculiarly Irish and may in fact be motivated less by cowardice than by a charitable desire not to unduly wound, nevertheless it is a pusillanimous one which merely serves to create and foster confusion and, in the end, tarnishes reputations unjustly. The truth must always be established, no matter what the outcome - let the chips fall where they may. Cover-ups are ultimately dishonourable and inevitably lead to the suspicion that an even greater can of worms is being concealed.

But the survivors of Jadotville must also bear some of the blame for this sorry fiasco. Their failure to speak out and defend themselves, their very silence in the face of intense critical speculation has merely fuelled the clouds of suspicion and innuendo which have hung over these events for the past thirty eight years.

It is one thing to accuse a man of dereliction of duty, to tease him for a lack of manliness even, to taunt him with being a fool or a dullard - it is altogether another to accuse him of cowardice, of failing to come to a comrade's rescue. That is simply too explosive an issue to be shelved and discarded in the hope that it will soon be conveniently forgotten.

The official history chooses to gloss over these issues, contenting itself with giving a sanitised version of the events involved. However, the stigma attached to Jadotville and Lufira cannot easily be cauterised by any lily-livered reluctance to grasp the nettle.

Perhaps even more telling, the failure to award any Distinguished Service Medals (DSMs) or any other awards for gallantry points up the official attitude towards Jadotville. It is quite simply inconceivable that, in probably the greatest-ever engagement involving Irish troops in battle, not one single solitary soldier merited an award for bravery.

Though many of the participants are now dead and buried, there is the reputation of the survivors still living to be considered, not to mention the morale and tradition of the army itself. Honour and the good name of the men involved demands no less than a full inquiry even at this late stage.

Chapter 2.A
Failure at Lufira Bridge

But what really happened during those terrible days leading up to the surrender in Jadotville and the ignominious imprisonment of the Irish garrison? What is the real truth behind the events which led to the failure to take and cross Lufira Bridge, the catalyst which was to lead directly to the Jadotville collapse?

In the absence of a first-hand chronicle of events by the principals involved on both sides, no historically accurate account can ever be produced, nonetheless it is possible to piece together a fairly accurate picture of the unfolding traumatic events based on both official and unofficial reports and reliable eye-witness accounts.

When the first attacks on the Irish troops began, the commander of C Company, Comdt. Pat Quinlan, quickly realised the danger and began to organise his defenses. With his back to Jadotville he dug in his men, harrying his commanders to get the trenches dug as quickly as possible in the classic formation. He was tireless in his zeal to ensure that every trench was properly placed to ensure the best fields of fire and supporting links wherever possible and that each was deep enough to afford complete protection from enemy fire. He exuded energy and confidence as if this was the moment he had been awaiting all his military life. Moreover, the troops were buoyed by their success in storming Gendarmerie HQ just a couple of weeks earlier.

His decision to take up position there has been criticised by the Military Adviser to the UN Secretary General, Indar Jit Rikhye, in his book "UN Peacekeeping on the Congo Crises," who says that "Quinlan had camped there for convenience and for quick access to the European quarter, in doing so he had ignored tactical considerations. The invitation was obviously a ruse to entrap UN troops."

Quinlan, however, always maintained that he had been directed to site there; his task had been to protect the inhabitants of Jadotville and there was no other alternative, he had merely occupied the area previously vacated by the Swedes.

Troops now fully deployed, the two armoured cars were placed in an enfilade position from where they could cut off infiltrating enemy attacks and provide full support to the crisscross of trenches. Radio communications, so vital to any defence, were established, supplies of ammunition and water checked, and the troops then settled down to face whatever the enemy might throw at them.

The first few attacks were desultory, more skirmishes than all-out assaults on the defending positions, then the Belgian mercenary commanders made a surprising gesture. In order to convince the Irish and UN HQs that surrender was the only realistic policy, they were now prepared to allow a deputation from the Jadotville garrison to travel back to Battalion HQ in Elizabethville to convey their message and to try to persuade the Irish troops to surrender.

Capt. Liam Donnelly, accompanied by an NCO and a driver, bravely volunteered to take a truck through enemy lines back to Elizabethville via Lufira bridge. Aware of the urgency of the situation, the group travelled as hard as they were able, arriving at the Irish camp just as the sun was about to set but then, to Donnelly's consternation, he was then left cooling his heels for five precious hours while the battalion brass entertained the UN supremo, Conor Cruise O'Brien, to dinner in the battalion mess.

And even when he did eventually get a hearing, he was amazed to discover no great urgency apparent. Neither the battalion staff officers, nor Cruise O'Brien himself, appeared to have fully grasped the gravity of the situation, leaving Donnelly almost in tears with frustration.

On his arrival once more back in Jadotville, without too

much to show for his efforts, Donnelly found the situation more grim than ever. The company was still surrounded, jeep loads of heavily-armed gendarmerie skirted the Irish positions aggressively, and the attitude of the Katangese left little doubt of their intentions to attack. This wasn't too long in coming.

The first real attack took place while most of the company were attending Mass. Gendarmes in jeeps and on foot swarmed into the Irish position expecting an easy victory but instead they found the trenches manned and were met with a hail of fire which broke their ranks in confusion.

Corporal John Monahan from Athlone led the defence. Returning from the wash-house in his singlet with his towel wrapped around his neck, he spotted the Katangese paras launching their attack during Mass. Without a second thought, he quickly got behind the Vickers machine gun and cut the enemy to pieces. Monahan later figured in another incident when Pte. Tahany, a young Sligo rifleman, was completely buried in a bomb attack on the weapons pit. Tahany was in total shock when he was pulled out, but Monahan took him under his wing for the rest of the fighting and he performed valiantly thereafter.

This spirited Irish defence must have come as a surprise to the attackers who had obviously been led by their Belgian advisers to believe that their assault would be a push-over. The defenders, they were told, were poorly-equipped with no prospect of escape and had only limited supplies of ammunition, food and water. Furthermore, the briefing went, the Irish were inexperienced in battle and if they didn't surrender in a very short time, could easily be overrun. At least that was the way the script was supposed to read - but the Irish soon added a couple of chapters of their own.

The heavy machine-guns of the armoured cars, with their superior firepower and longer range, chattered their deadly staccato message as the confused enemy retired to lick his wounds, regroup, and prepare for the next assault. The defenders now had cause to be thankful for the long hours of training back home in Ireland and for the sometimes tedious persistence of their conscientious commander in carrying out realistic exercises while other units lolled in the sun.

For the next five days and nights, wave after wave of attacks made life a living hell for the harassed defenders. A continuous hail of fire poured down on the trenches, keeping the defenders pinned down and making movement outside impossible. Mortar shells burst all round them but by sheer good fortune none scored a direct hit on any trench which would certainly have spelled curtains for everyone inside.

An Irishman working with Union Miniere based in Jadotville, a Mr. Kearney, now estimated enemy strength at between four and five thousand troops. On July 15th alone, at least ten separate attacks by up to sixty strong were beaten off. Occasionally, during short lulls in the fighting, the defenders could see bodies being dragged away by the Katangese but then the attacks would start again and there would be no further time for detached observation.

Exploding mortar shells from the Irish 60mm mortar destroyed a nearby garage and wrecked some surrounding buildings, causing a fierce blaze which lit up the night scene in a macabre light. Slowly, inexorably, Irish casualties mounted. First two, then three, then five men fell badly wounded, and only prompt and efficient medical aid managed to save their lives though evacuation was impossible.

Soon afterwards, Irish morale received a major boost. Accurate fire by the mortars targeted an enemy assembly area, and a direct hit on an ammunition dump sent exploding shells whizzing in all directions to the accompaniment of loud cheers from the trenches. The dump blazed furiously all night long and into the next day. This was a major stroke of luck since the dump contained most of the shells for a French-made 75mm gun which could have knocked out both armoured cars and devastated the Irish position if left to its own devices. The 75mm gun crew were also killed in the blast.

The enemy now managed to capture a house about 150 yards from Coy HQ from where it completely pinned down troops manning the forward trenches. It was therefore essential that this position be neutralised and, under covering fire from the trenches, an anti-tank section commanded by Cpl. Monaghan raced into open ground to engage the position with a 84mm recoilless rifle, completely destroying the house and killing all the enemy.

Monahan later provided a moment of light relief during a brief lull in the fighting, which lifted everybody's spirits. Turning to A Coy platoon commander, Lt. Joe Leech, lying exhausted in the trench beside him, he handed him a piece of paper, murmuring politely "Sign this please sir".

Without thinking, Joe reached for the piece of paper and was about to sign when suddenly he happened to glance at its contents. It was an application for leave, printed on official army paper, made out for a weekend pass at a holiday camp in Elizabethville!

Letting out a roar, Joe chased a laughing Monahan out of the trench and across open ground, almost turning the air blue as he went, and then everybody burst out laughing at the sheer coolness of the man in the face of such pressure. Both returned arm-in-arm to cheers from the trenches.

Besides the lack of 81mm mortars which turned out to be a major blunder, the defenders also suffered from the lack of a sniper who could take out key members of enemy units as the occasion demanded, such as his mortars, anti-tank and HQ. The enemy mortar crews in particular were very professional, being in the main Belgian or French paratroopers, but C/S Prendergast, an All-Army champion rifle marksman, more than made up for the absence of a sniper by taking out several members of the mortar crews with his FN rifle. Pte Stanley from Tullamore also distinguished himself behind his Bren gun, not to mention CQMS Neville who heroically ensured an adequate supply of food under most adverse conditions.

Concerned at the build-up of enemy forces and the consequent drain on supplies of food, water and ammunition, Quinlan again radioed HQ in Elizabethville for help, but radio contact was very patchy due to the noise of battle and the failure of most of the sets to operate properly at such long range.

The situation was urgent, he declared, and unless reinforcements arrived pretty soon, the defenders were in grave danger of being wiped out. He was therefore gratified to learn that a relief force of about company strength would shortly be on its way, supported by two armoured cars and two Swedish armoured personnel carriers (APCs).

This news greatly heartened the defenders, raising their morale and encouraging their will to resist, but it also had the effect of redoubling the fury of the attackers. The Belgian mercenaries were able to intercept messages between the Irish units on their more powerful radios even though these were relayed through the medium of Irish, and they now decided to head off the reinforcements at Lufira Bridge, the only point at which a crossing was possible. A smaller railway bridge was also situated a short distance away downstream but this was not deemed fordable.

Arriving at Lufira Bridge the Irish relief party, code-named Force Kane One after its artillery corps commander, Lt. Col. Johnny Kane, carried out a hurried recce and decided that there was no other possible way to cross in force except by the bridge. But because the light was fading fast, he now decided that the attack would have to be made in the dark and, under covering fire, two APCs (Armoured Personnel Carriers) made their way onto the narrow structure, supported by infantrymen on foot.

The enemy had driven a bulldozer onto the bridge, blocking one side completely, and had also littered the bridge with concrete-filled barrels, tree stumps, and other heavy objects. Now one of the Irish armoured cars attempted to nudge the bulldozer over the side of the bridge into the river. A hail of small-arms fire greeted them from the opposite bank, causing some panic and confusion, and in the ensuing melee one of the cars stalled in the middle of the bridge, its axle trapped on a barrel.

Bravely defying enemy fire, Gunner Murphy from Ballincollig dashed from the safety of his APC and after a herculean effort managed to dislodge the barrel, freeing the axle and enabling the APC to withdraw.

Taken aback by the unexpected strength of enemy fire and fearing an anti-tank attack or, worse still, the demolition of the bridge itself by explosives, the OC gave the order to withdraw from the safety of his APC, and this led to an angry altercation between himself and Mark Carroll, the commander of the cavalry armoured cars.

Carroll, furious at the apparent indecision, climbed out from the protection of his own armoured car to direct the evacuation in person, which by then was in complete confusion. Finally both cars managed to withdraw with their protecting infantry cover intact and the situation was hastily reviewed. A decision was then taken to abandon the attempt to cross the bridge until the next day, and the force then retired to a position about six kilometres away to bed down for the night and prepare for a dawn attack the following morning.

But by next morning the situation was beyond redemption. During the night the enemy had moved up fresh troops which ensured that any attempt to force a crossing would be costly indeed in terms of casualties. Also, for some strange reason the rescue force was not in position to attack the bridge till as late as 08.30 hours, which delay ensured that the element of surprise was completely lost.

All attempts to approach the bridge were now met with heavy enemy fire and shortly afterwards the nearby railway bridge was blown. The rescue attempt was finally abandoned and the tired and dispirited troops of Force Kane One returned to Elizabethville on Sept 14.

Chapter 3.A
Force Kane Two

Two days later, at first light on the 16th, yet another rescue attempt was planned. This time the force was strengthened by a company of Ghurkas under Major Mangla. Again the timing was poor. Originally due to arrive at Lufira bridge at approximately 0530 hours, it signally failed to do so possibly due to the fact that some of the troops were being carried in converted buses, many of which were in poor shape.

A Fouga jet fighter also made travelling hazardous by its bombing and strafing raids on the column, obliging them to take evasive action whenever it appeared. Only one Irish soldier was wounded by shrapnel, but their Ghurka comrades were not so lucky - their casualties numbered three killed and five wounded. Every attempt by the force to approach the vicinity of the bridge met with withering enemy fire, and it soon became obvious that the enemy position had been heavily reinforced during the night. Armoured car and APC fire was directed onto the bridge area, plus mortar and MMG fire, but to no avail.

It soon became apparent that a daylight attack without air support would almost certainly incur heavy casualties which would seriously endanger attempts to extricate the garrison at Jadotville and bring them back safely through Lufira. Reluctantly, a decision was taken to abandon the rescue and at 16.30 hours the force returned again to Elizabethville. Their return journey was severely hampered by the strafing runs of the Fouga and during an ambush five Irish and five Ghurkas were wounded. Some shells then exploded which killed a further two Ghurkas and injured ten more.

Happy to hear that no rescue was now likely, the Katangese

commanders around Jadotville moved up more and more troops until the build-up signified that an all-out assault was imminent. Water was now becoming a major worry for the defenders. Urgent radio messages were sent to HQ requesting that supplies be air-dropped if at all possible.

Soon afterwards the defenders were heartened to see a lone helicopter appear which, after circling for a while, crash-landed among the Irish lines. Cpl. Bobby Allen and Pte. Pat Neville did heroic work trying to direct it to land in the correct area, but it suffered severe damage and was unable to take off again.

The brave Norwegian pilot, Bjorne Hovden, who had come from the Antarctic to volunteer for the job, stayed with the Irish in their trenches right to the bitter end and was of considerable help to them while in captivity, raising morale and rallying their sagging spirits.

Alas, the water he brought was contained in oily jerricans and was of such poor quality as to be almost useless. To add to their woes, bombing and strafing attacks by a Fouga jet fighter now became a regular feature of daily life, yet another hazard in the ever-increasing volume of attacks by the enemy.

Another example of great bravery springs to mind. The defenders remember with gratitude the wonderful little Belgian lady whose house lay right in the middle of the defensive zone. This brave woman plied them with home-made cakes and scones and attempted to lighten their load during their darkest hours.

Meanwhile, back in Elizabethville, urgent requests to the British to allow UN planes to use Manono airport to relieve the beleaguered garrison were refused. This almost unbelievably hostile action appears to have been influenced by considerable British interest in seeing the UN mission in Katanga fail. Enemy troops now threatened to infiltrate the forward defensive positions, and two men from Athlone, Butch Brennan and John Gorman bravely volunteered to man an isolated machine-gun emplacement dug in on the side of an ant-hill dominating the approaches, and there they stayed till the very end, their covering fire sealing any possible enemy breach.

As the fifth day of the siege dawned, the weary, exhausted defenders, by now aware that the rescue attempt had been abandoned, slumped in their trenches to await the final assault which they knew must be surely imminent. Their thoughts were with their kinfolk back at home, fully convinced they might never set eyes on them again.

The situation was clearly desperate. The men had had no proper sleep for five days and nights, while the intense tropical heat was also taking its toll. Swarms of insects buzzed incessantly around the stinking trenches; food, water and ammunition supplies were almost completely expended. All that was left to eat were some crumpled dog-biscuits, while the water, the precious, life-giving water, was by now stagnant and was making the men sick.

The enemy was also growing increasingly confident, despite suffering heavy casualties. The defenders could clearly hear their shouted threats to kill and eat them as soon as they were captured, which clearly didn't help boost morale.

The Fouga jet fighter again made its low-flying appearance to strafe the trenches, but this time it was met with a hail of concentrated small-arms fire which damaged it and forced it to fly away, ensuring all future bombing attacks had to be made from a far greater height. The radio messages appealing for help reflected the defenders' desperation but now, to add to their problems, the 31 sets began to fail badly, with only the occasional garbled message getting through. None of the replies afforded any consolation.

What dreadful thoughts must have gone through their minds, sitting there in their stinking muddy holes, reeking of sweat, putrid water and rotting food, the smell of faeces and urine mingling with the acrid odour of cordite in the air. Silent, heartfelt prayers were offered up, about the only consolation in their hour of need. Was this finally the end of the line? Was this how their glorious adventure of peace, embarked upon with such hopeful bravado, was to end, spilling their life-blood in the rich red soil of the Congo?

But still they fought on, those gallant men of the West, their courage never wavering, resolved to go down bravely in hand-to-hand fighting if need be when the trenches were finally over-run. This was the moment of truth, the moment for which every soldier prepares, but which he hopes and prays will never arrive.

But then, in the midst of despair, as if in answer to their prayers, out of the blue came a surprising offer from the Belgians, an offer which sent renewed hope surging through their veins. The Irish position was obviously hopeless, they were told, but it was not the Belgians' intention, nor indeed their wish, to inflict further hardship and casualties on the defenders who had fought as bravely as any group of men could rightly have been expected to.

This first offer was quickly rejected, but then back came a further, more interesting offer from the Belgians which this time was given careful consideration by the Irish commander. If the Irish would agree to a cease-fire, the attackers would agree to withdraw from around the Irish defensive positions, water supplies would be re-connected, and joint patrols of Irish and Katangese troops would be operated to maintain order in the town.

If, however, they refused, they would be attacked with more troops and heavier firepower until they were finally over-whelmed, and this time their safety could not be guaranteed. It was Hobson's Choice, a decision which Quinlan alone could make.

Before making that momentous decision, however, one upon which so many lives depended, he consulted with his commanders as to the choices open to him. These revealed little or no room for manouevre. They had no further communication with the outside world, and had little or no hope of escape or rescue; ammunition supplies were exhausted, their food and water were all gone, and the men were completely out on their feet. The picture was gloomy indeed.

At long last Quinlan took his lonely decision, the most important of his entire life. The safety of his men came foremost, he decided. Reluctantly, he resolved to bite the bullet and accept terms, a decision which was to eventually result in the safe return to Ireland of all his men but one which was to damn him with faint praise for the rest of his army career.

Signals were sent to the Belgians that their offer would be accepted and a delegation left to negotiate with the Burgomaster and the OC Gendarmerie. But shortly after that, pressure was put on Quinlan to abandon the trenches and move into a hotel in Jadotville with all their weapons being housed elsewhere. It was obvious that this was tantamount to surrender but there was very little option but to comply, despite the fact that some of the Irish still wanted to fight on. They considered that they, and not the Katangese, had won the battle, but they were soon prevailed upon to comply.

The mood was sombre. Besides the obvious relief at having their lives spared, there was a certain sadness at leaving the trenches where they had made their gallant stand, the feeling of a job left undone, of abandoning something half-way through. Documentation was now destroyed and some heavier weapons rendered unserviceable to prevent their use by the enemy.

The attitude of the Belgian paratroopers and mercenaries was surprisingly friendly, many of them complimenting the Irish on the bravery and tenacity of their defence. But the native Katangese, who had suffered severe casualties, were far more hostile, and it came as no surprise when several days later the camp was surrounded by a large force and all their arms confiscated. Effectively they were now prisoners-of-war.

However, since the UN was by now involved and the matter had become an international incident, there didn't seem much point in making their disarming an issue so they reluctantly went along with the process. Later on in discussions with the Belgians, it transpired that they firmly believed that the Irish had suffered heavy casualties and were keen to know how they had managed to dispose of the bodies. They flatly refused to believe that no Irish soldier had been killed and only a handful injured.

They were especially amazed that no severe Irish casualties were sustained during the sustained bombardment by enemy mortars. This can only be explained by the design of the defender's trenches which were built up rather than down, as is the norm. Because of the looseness of the Congo soil, it was impossible to dig down and shore up the sides of the trenches, instead the loose soil was thrown up and packed high all around the trench to give protection from enemy shrapnel. It was also lucky that no trench sustained a direct hit from mortar shells which of course would have meant curtains for its occupants.

Enemy casualties had been severe. One Belgian estimate revealed that about thirty white mercenaries had perished in the attack because that number of coffins had been buried and only whites merited coffins, and that between 150 and 300 Katangese troops had been killed and several hundred more wounded.

Severe as these figures might seem at first glance, it must be remembered that the Irish were experienced, well-trained troops, well dug-in and superbly led, with machine-gun and light mortar support. The armoured cars alone expended over 17,500 rounds of heavy machine-gun ammo, which was bound to have a devastating effect on attackers with no protective armour.

As for the suggestion that the defenders might have broken out and make good their escape, this theory does not stand up to serious analysis. Even assuming that they might have actually got through the surrounding enemy cordon, they would then have merely been sitting ducks for the Fouga jet in the open, without adequate supplies of food and water and, above all, no transport.

Chapter 4.A
Passing the Buck

Over the years, those who took part in the battle for Jadotville and the failed attempt at Lufira Bridge have been noticeably reluctant to discuss the affair. In the absence of positive facts, every effort seems to have been made by their compatriots to spare them possible embarrassment. Other military engagements are freely discussed and exploits boasted about by troops who served in the Congo - the Tunnel, the taking of the Airport, the capture of Gendarme HQ - but never Jadotville. This is still a no-go area.

In time Quinlan was promoted to Lieutenant Colonel and eventually to full Colonel, but he never again attained any command of real significance and never again served overseas, though the army authorities stoutly maintain there has never been a blot on his official record. In time he became the butt of sly jokes, the target of critical remarks in the bars, tainted with the cruelly contemptuous soubriquet of 'Jadotville Jack'. Only twice more did he again get a chance to show his true mettle.

This occurred during a riot on the border near Castleblayney, when a number of troops were disarmed by a hostile mob, mainly women. The situation looked like developing into a rout until, rather reluctantly, Quinlan was given command of a batch of fresh troops and sent in to quell the situation. Typically, he dismounted the troops en route and gave them a quick introduction into the mechanics of riot control and how he wanted the job done. The result was that the mob was quickly and firmly put to flight and the situation once again put under control.

Somewhat surprisingly, perhaps, those under his command in Jadotville have never openly criticised him or undermined his decision to surrender, and the spontaneous ecstatic reception he received in Athlone on their return could scarcely have been possible if there were any doubts as to his courage and the correctness of his decision. It is an army truism that the enlisted men are rarely wrong in their assessment of an officer.

Quinlan's decision to surrender, which was ultimately his alone, appears in hindsight to have been the correct, indeed the only possible one. This is not simply because his surrender succeeded in saving the lives of himself and his men, but that he acted with the best interests of his troops at heart, probably against his better instincts. Having fought so long and valiantly, it would have been nothing short of criminal if he had needlessly and vain-gloriously decided to endanger his troops' lives by refusing the honourable terms offered and fighting on instead.

The other came when he assumed command of the defence of Collins Barracks against a marauding mob which marched from a demonstration in O'Connell Street up along the quays to mass menacingly outside the main gates, demanding arms to go and defend the beseiged Catholics in Northern Ireland, led a young firebrand student from Cork who afterwards rose to become a prominent government minister. The situation looked so bad that some young officers mounted a machine gun on a roof overlooking the gates, but then Quinlan arrived and by his prompt and decisive actions quickly got the situation under control.

The brashness of youth sometimes blinds us to the grim realities of life and the harsh decisions which command of men entails. Today, there are very few army people who still believe Quinlan's decision to surrender was wrong, though pockets of hostility still linger here and there throughout the army.

It is understandable too that the survivors failed to get their point of view across on their return to Ireland. No one in the army wanted to know; the official attitude was to let the matter die, the sooner forgotten about the better. In any case, further in-depth analysis might only have uncovered an even greater can of worms and no one was anxious to cause further embarrassment.

It is true that there are still those, some of them survivors of Jadotville, who continue to believe that the garrison ought never have surrendered, having won the firefight, but they are few and far between. Most of those who opposed Quinlan's decision now agree it was the right one, indeed the only possible one.

But even now, when it is generally acknowledged that a grave injustice has been perpetrated, no one high up in the army seems to have the will to press for an enquiry. If they did, it surely must be that somebody in authority would have the courage to take the first step.

Looking back dispassionately across a thirty-eight year divide, some things now appear crystal clear. The blame for the disasters at Jadotville and Lufira, and disasters they truly were, must be laid squarely, not at the feet of the defenders of Jadotville, but at the would-be rescuers at Lufira Bridge and those in command further back in Battalion and UN HQ.

It is patently clear that, far from showing the white feather, far from refusing to battle on, the troops in Jadotville had fought bravely almost to the last gasp in defence of their position. After all a total of five dead and thirty-one wounded is not exactly a tea-party. The accusing finger for failure must be pointed elsewhere.

First and foremost, UN Command was naive in the extreme in sending only one company of Irish troops out to an isolated post such as Jadotville, without any supporting armour and with insufficient transport. Only a short time before, the Swedes had pulled out their two companies of troops on the grounds that it was impossible to defend the area with such a small number of men. It is almost certain that UN HQ were duped by the Belgians into sending troops to Jadotville where they could later be used as a bargaining ploy.

UN HQ in Leopoldville was also culpable in ordering the Irish to attack the Gendarmerie Headquarters and then shortly afterwards nullifying the result, especially after the Irish had successfully captured it. This played right into the hands of Tshombe and his Belgian advisers. Had the arms and ammunition captured in the raid, practically their entire stock, been withheld, no further hostile actions could henceforth have been undertaken. The decision to return the gendarmerie weapons displayed gross political naivete on the part of the UN supremo, Conor Cruise O'Brien and his military advisers, led by Maj. Gen. Sean McKeown, who did not appear to be fully briefed about the hostile intentions of the Katangese. Intelligence reports were apparently almost non-existent.

In his book, To Katanga and Back, Cruise O'Brien appears to gloss over the incident, giving it a bare mention as if it was something of a sideshow to matters of greater import. But it is fair to say that were it not for the determination and bravery of the defenders at Jadotville, a catastrophe of titanic proportions would have occurred which no amount of glossing or obfuscation could have avoided.

Rikhye also harshly criticises Cruise O'Brien for naivete. "As to the fate of the Irish in Jadotville, O'Brien had ignored the correct advice he had been given by Raja not to send a company of infantry off on its own, given the hostility with the Katangese and their European mercenaries."

And when the balloon really went up in Jadotville, with the real risk of the position being over-run and countless Irish lives lost, helicopters and fighter planes should immediately have been sent to the rescue. True, Cruise O'Brien did request fighter bombers to counter enemy air superiority but these were not forthcoming.

Pressure should been have applied on the British to support the UN action and make Manono airport available. It scarcely seems possible that UN HQ did not fully appreciate how serious the situation really was.

But a large proportion of the blame must also be apportioned to those in command of 31st Irish Battalion at HQ in Elizabethville. They knew, or ought to have known, the desperate situation in Jadotville and acted more vigorously to prevent C Company being over-run. Their action in keeping a frustrated Capt. Donnelly waiting five hours while they wined and dined the UN supremo certainly takes some explaining. In addition, ten days supply of American pack rations were left behind at Elizabethville on the basis of delivery as soon as possible on transport availability. Such rations were never delivered, another example of woeful bungling in Battalion HQ.

It is strangely moving, even at this late stage, to read through the historic radio messages which streamed between Elizabethville and Jadotville, to follow the increasingly desperate tone of the exchanges, garbled though they are. Additionally, one can only wonder at the inexplicable differences between the official version and the original record, which suggests possible tampering and in itself alone might well justify an inquiry.

Fate plays strange tricks. It is surely ironic in the extreme that Lt. Col. McNamee, the battalion commander who replaced the original commander, should have been one of those at the receiving end of the infamous 'Sir Patrick Murphy' incident which took place in Galway, while Quinlan, now desperately depending on him for help out in Jadotville, was none other than the very man who had landed him in the soup. By such quirks is history made topical.

This incident occurred at a St. Patrick's Day function in the officers mess in Renmore, attended by a number of local dignatories and the press. 'Sir Patrick', who passed himself off as a member of the Coldstream Guards but was later exposed as a conman, proposed a toast in the bar to An tUachtaran (the President), to which everyone present drank. But then OC An Cead Cath committed a major gaffe.

Well fortified with refreshments and keen to reciprocate cordiality, he foolishly arose and proposed a toast to the Queen. This flummoxed most of those present, who were clearly at a loss how to react - all except Quinlan, who objected violently and swore he would 'drink to no damn

Queen'. This was too good a scoop for an alert local journalist to miss.

The resultant uproar in the national press led to an official inquiry, and a court martial on an unconnected minor charge saw Lt. Col. Dinny Houston relieved of his command and sent to Cork, while a number of other officers, McNamee included, were reprimanded. While it is perhaps unfair to allow conjecture to run loose, McNamee would scarcely have been human if he hadn't at some stage allowed himself a fleeting moment of unholy glee at seeing the prickly Quinlan caught in a proper stew out in Jadotville, forced to depend on one of the very men he had shafted to rescue him.

No explanation has ever been given either for the inexplicable disappearance of a personal letter sent by Quinlan to his wife, given to journalist John Ross when he visited him in captivity, which contained an original copy of a page of the wireless messages passed between Jadotville and Battalion HQ during the battle. Ross apparently mentioned this letter at HQ but was then persuaded to hand it over and assured by the OC that he would personally ensure its delivery. It was never delivered, which only serves to harden suspicions that it was deliberately opened and suppressed because of fears that its contents might prove compromising.

Chapter 5.A
Jadotville Jack

But part of the problem had its origins in the selection of commanders. The battalion's original OC in the Congo was unceremoniously stripped of his command after only a few months because of incompetence. And most of the rest of the force commanders, while undoubtedly willing and conscientious, had been far too long removed from first-hand participation with fighting troops and active service conditions.

Thus the selection process was deeply flawed. It seems crazy that people should have been appointed who had little or no recent experience of commanding fighting men. It is simply asking too much of those who have been well 'dug-in' in cushy administration jobs all their lives to suddenly transform themselves into so many Hercules at one fell swoop.

Many of those in charge were beyond the age of active soldiering, some indeed had not commanded troops in the field for many years past. Even worse, some were not suited to serve in the field under any circumstances, due to personal problems such as addiction to alcohol. Had nothing untoward occurred they just might have been lucky enough to get away with it, as others had before them, but this is a luxury that cannot be indulged when men's lives are at stake.

The folly of this type of policy is there for all to see yet, even today, present policy is geared to take such a system a step further. Now desk-wallahs have been allowed to re-write the promotion rules to favour themselves by perpetuating the promotion of officers to the highest echelons of the army who have no experience at all of leading fighting troops, to the exclusion of those who have commanded troops in the field. One can only shudder at future possible consequences.

But this kind of behaviour is nothing new. Throughout history, desk-wallahs have always contrived to re-write promotion rules to favour their particular ilk, putting one in mind of W.S. Gilbert's famous 1879 libretto from the operetta H.M.S. Pinafore:

> "Stick close to your desks
> And never go to sea,
> And you all may be rulers
> Of the Queen's Navee!"

The commander of the rescue missions, Force Kane One and Two, which foundered at Lufira Bridge, cannot escape criticism either. The failure to take the bridge and effect a crossing was crucial to the ability of the Jadotville garrison to hold out. Had this rescue force got through, their supplies and added manpower would have given the defenders' morale an incalculable boost, enabling them to mount a proper defence and possibly even to break out.

Most official reports of Lufira indicate that enemy fire from the opposite bank had pinned the attackers down, but a study of the available maps and intelligence reports show clearly that, far from being dominated by the opposite bank, in fact the Irish side of the river had a definite height advantage over the enemy side. It should therefore have been possible to pin the enemy down with accurate covering fire during the first rescue attempt and then mount a determined assault across the river on either side of the bridge, perhaps under cover of a smoke screen. The enemy strength at that time would almost certainly have been unable to withstand such an assault.

There can be no questioning the courage of the Irish troops, but questions can, and must, be put about the levels of commitment and determination which existed among the higher ranks, in particular Force Kane. There is clear evidence of dithering, of a lack of resolution, in the decision to withdraw six kilometres away to bed down for the night without maintaining contact with the enemy, thus giving him a free hand to wire the bridges for demolition and to reinforce his position.

Knowing the desperate situation pertaining in Jadotville, with the lives of their comrades depending on their actions, a far more determined initial effort at rescue might surely have been expected rather than simply waiting till next morning to attack, and, this attack having failed, returning home tamely to base. Why did this attack not take place at first light, as planned? This delay was probably crucial.

The rescue force commander, Lt. Col. Kane, may well have been counted as fortunate not to have been court-martialled over his performance, as indeed might some members of battalion HQ as well. UN HQ, in particular O'Brien and McKeown, must also be indicted for failing to inform the garrison in Jadotville that they were part of Morthor, the UN overall plan of campaign. As it was, the defenders knew nothing of any plan right up till the day the assault on their position commenced. Dag Hammarskjold's instructions to O'Brien were, according to Brian Urquhart in his book "Hammarskjold", designed to get the UN, and particularly O'Brien and the UN Katanga command, out of an impossible situation "into which they had fallen through military and other forms of incompetence."

Some criticism of the chaplain's role in Jadotville has also been voiced from time to time. It scarcely needs to be said that assembling troops for mass at a moment of great danger reflects poorly on his judgement and indirectly on that of the company commander as well, who, after all, had direct overall responsibility for the security of the position.

As for Jadotville itself, the final word has yet to be written. But justice demands no less than that all those brave men of C Company be given the honours and acclamation, however belatedly, that they so richly deserve - men like Liam Donnelly, John Monaghan, Bobby Allen, medic Pte Broderick, and Gunner Murphy from Ballincollig amongst many others.

It is hard to escape the conclusion that the Jadotville garrison were 'hung out to dry', that they were the victims of a cynical manoeuvre on the part of the Katangese and the Belgians to isolate and capture the company. Inexperience or ineptitude on the part of the United Nations Commission in the Congo very nearly consigned them to a dreadful fate, worse even than the deaths and mutilation suffered in the Niemba massacre. Small wonder they remain bitter about their treatment.

Additionally, those civilians who bravely risked their lives to assist the Irish, notably the heroic Norwegian pilot who volunteered to fly an unserviceable helicopter to bring water to the Jadotville trenches, the little Belgian woman with the cakes, and the Irishman in the town who supplied valuable intelligence on enemy dispositions should, if still alive, be publicly decorated for their bravery. Their contribution to date has been callously ignored.

It has been posited that gallantry awards cannot, and should not, be given to those who surrender in battle. That position is not tenable under the peculiar circumstances of the battle of Jadotville. Awards for gallantry are made on an individual basis for bravery, irrespective of the outcome of any battle, and many such cases are recorded in the annals of other armies in major battles throughout history.

In November 1998, bravery medals were awarded to many of those who served in the Congo, particularly those who fell in Niemba and whose service had previously been ignored, thereby removing a painful thorn which had lodged in the sides of survivors and their relatives for many years. Yet incredibly the survivors of Jadotville continue to be ignored, a situation which simply cannot be allowed to stand unchallenged.

But above all, the army should acknowledge the unjustified slur cast on a brave and prudent officer, the commander at Jadotville, Comdt. Pat Quinlan, whose outstanding leadership under fire did so much to bring his men safely through their ordeal. Sadly, he passed away in 1997, before he could establish his innocence of any wrong-doing.

225

True, the Military College belatedly commissioned a study of the campaign in 1993 as part of the 50th Command & Staff Course, but their conclusions were so lack-lustre and their failure to grasp the nettle and properly apportion blame so patently weak-kneed, that their report can only be seen as an exercise in semantics and virtually worthless. Little wonder that the townspeople of Athlone, well briefed by their menfolk, turned out in such large numbers to give Quinlan a hero's welcome on his return home.

It matters not a whit that he was prickly and sharp-tongued, that he was impetuous, that he rubbed people up the wrong way, that he drank too much for his own good, that his gung-ho attitude irritated a lot of his fellow officers from time to time. What matters is what he did, or did not do, when his moment of truth arrived.

He might perhaps be subject to criticism for his naivete in believing the terms of the surrender agreement to be honourable, for being duped. The subsequent surrender must indeed have been galling in the extreme, but I have spoken to no-one who fought in Jadotville who still criticises his decision to surrender.

The army should now belatedly swallow its pride and publicly honour Col. Pat Quinlan and all those brave men of C Company under his command who performed so gallantly under fire in Jadotville. The bar-room soubriquet of 'Jadotville Jack', heretofore employed as a measure of contempt, may in time come to stand for honour, courage, and the willingness to fight.